KIDNAPPED
IN THE
AMAZON
JUNGLE

KIDNAPPED
IN THE
AMAZON
JUNGLE

F. BRUCE LAMB
MANUEL CÓRDOVA-RIOS

illustrated by
CLAIRE COTTS

North Atlantic Books
Berkeley, California

Published by
North Atlantic Books,
P.O. Box 12327
Berkeley, California 94701

Cover and book design by Paula Morrison
Printed in the United States of America by Malloy Lithographing

Kidnapped in the Amazon Jungle is sponsored by the Society for the Study of Native Arts and Sciences, a nonprofit educational corporation whose goals are to develop an educational and crosscultural perspective linking various scientific, social, and artistic fields; to nurture a holistic view of arts, sciences, humanities, and healing; and to publish and distribute literature on the relationship of mind, body, and nature.

Library of Congress Cataloging-in-Publication Data

Lamb, F. Bruce (Frank Bruce), 1913–1993
    Kidnapped in the Amazon Jungle / F. Bruce Lamb and Manuel Córdova-Rios.
       p. cm.
     ISBN 1–55643–173–2 (trade)
     1. Córdova-Rios, Manuel, 1887–1978.   2. Indians of South America—Peru—Amazonas—Captivities.   3. Indians of South America—Peru—Amazonas—Social life and customs.   4. Ayahuasca—Peru—Amazonas.   5. Hallucinogenic drugs and religious experience—Peru—Amazonas. I. Córdova-Rios, Manuel, 1887–1978.   II. Title.
F3429.1.A43C675 1994
615.8'82'092—dc20
[B]
                                                     93–44837
                                                     CIP

1   2   3   4   5   6   7   8   9 / 98   97   96   95   94

Contents

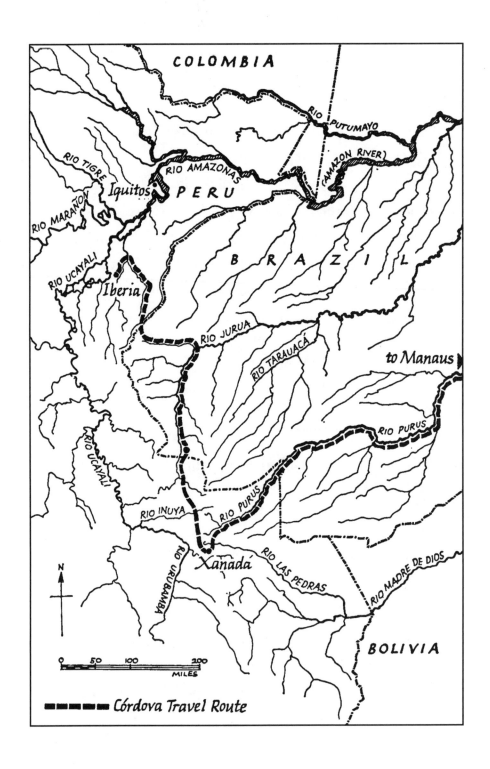

COLOMBIA

RIO PUTUMAYO

(AMAZON RIVER)

RIO TIGRE

RIO AMAZONAS

Iquitos

PERU

RIO MARAÑON

B R A Z I L

RIO UCAYALI

Iberia

RIO JURUA

RIO TARAUACÁ

to Manaus

RIO PURUS

RIO UCAYALI

RIO INUYA

RIO PURUS

RIO PURUS

RIO LAS PEDRAS

RIO MADRE DE DIOS

Xanadá

N

RIO URUBAMBA

50   100   200
MILES

BOLIVIA

████ ████ ████ Córdova Travel Route

Foreword

A FEELING OF awe is the first reaction of a newcomer entering the lush tropical forest of the Amazon. Constant hot weather and high rainfall all year in this equatorial zone provide an ideal setting for a great variety of plants and animals. They all grow together in a wild exuberant mixture. The exotic sounds, smells, and sights bring a feeling of mystery and strangeness to the outsider on a first visit. I, myself, still have this feeling on coming back after a long absence, even though I have spent many months in the various tropical forests of South America, West Africa, and Asia.

The Amazon is the largest river in the world. It has no rivals. By comparison, the Mississippi, the Nile, and the Congo are small. Thousands of smaller streams gather their waters from a vast tropical forest and flow into the Amazon. As you would expect, this forest is also the largest area of tropical vegetation in the world, covering some three million square miles of land in five adjoining countries of South America: Brazil, Colombia, Ecuador, Peru, and Bolivia. There is a great cry of alarm in the world today over the rate at which the forests of the Amazon region are being destroyed by man.

The Spanish conquistador Francisco de Orellana first navigated the river in 1540. Coming down from Ecuador, he went all the way to the river's mouth on the Atlantic seacoast. Since then, many people have had strange adventures in this region, including the American president Theodore Roosevelt who nearly lost his life on one of the Amazon tributaries now named after him.

Exploration of the Amazon Valley by outsiders was mostly confined to the main rivers until the time of the rubber boom that began around 1850 and lasted until 1920. World demand for rubber used to make automobile tires and other modern items caused a great invasion of the Amazon forest. The rubber came from latex extracted from the bark of several different kinds of trees found scattered in the forest. The following story takes place as a result of this invasion of the Amazon jungle.

Even though the forest is dense and often difficult to penetrate, plants and animals of any one kind are usually not found close to each other. Men searching for rubber trees from which to get the latex that hardened into rubber had to go great distances into the forest in their quest. And in doing this, they soon came in conflict with the native Indians living there. This difficult situation is the background for Manuel Córdova's story.

When I went to Peru in the 1960s to make a timber survey of the upper Amazon area, Manuel Córdova was assigned to me as a guide. What follows is the story he told me of his life in the forest as a young man during the rubber boom days.

F. Bruce Lamb
Santa Fe, New Mexico

1

Jungle Rubber Camps

I Learn the Rubber Trade

MY MOTHER OBJECTED. She said that it was too dangerous for a boy of my age to go off into the jungle with men tapping rubber. Maybe she was right, the way it all turned out.

I was twelve, and had already been through all the school that existed in Iquitos, a small town on the banks of the Amazon River in Peru, South America. In Iquitos there was nothing much for me to do but run in the streets and play soccer with the other kids. My older sister Mariana didn't think that was good enough. She and her husband Lino were visiting our family. Finally, after much gentle per-susasion, they convinced my mother that I should go upriver with them to their rubber trading post above Iquitos and learn the boom-ing rubber business.

I, Manuel Córdova, was of course raring to go. It sounded like adventure to me. So we went upriver by launch to Iberia where Lino had his riverbank post. From there he sent groups of men off into the forest to set up rubber camps. I spent several weeks learning how the trading post operated, weighing in large balls of smoked rubber, and outfitting the rubber cutters with the supplies they needed for their work in the forest.

Then Lino suggested that I go out to one of the camps to learn the forest end of the business. There Roque, one of Lino's best men, could show me firsthand the ins and outs of a jungle rubber camp. I could learn how a group of tappers gathered latex from the trees along trails through the forest and smoked it into large rubber balls back at camp.

It took us several days paddling our canoe up a small stream deep in the jungle to reach the rubber camp. I learned a lot on that trip about how to make camp in the forest and hunt wild game for our meals. Finally we reached the rubber camp itself, which sat on the riverbank in a small clearing. It was made up of several palm-thatched shelters, each set on a pole framework, with dirt floors and no walls. We slept in hammocks hung from the rafters.

I spent a few days in camp learning how it operated. Roque took me into the forest to show me how they hunted game for our cooking fire. I learned many new things about life in the forest. So far life in the jungle didn't seem too dangerous to me. I didn't see what my mother had been so worried about.

Soon Roque decided that it was time for me to go out on the forest trails with the rubber tappers to see how they did their work. The men went out early in the morning, and it was dark and misty in the jungle until the sun came up. Even then, it seemed dark in the dense forest, because not much sunlight reached the ground.

One day when I was out with Jose, I was ahead on the trail looking for game to shoot. Some strangeness, a momentary feeling of something unusual about the jungle, stopped me in my tracks. I looked around from the spot where I stood on the faint shadowy rubber cutter's trail. In one hand I lightly held a shotgun, hoping to shoot a jungle partridge for the cooking fire back at camp. So I was alert to any sound that might indicate the presence of game.

Light and shadow played on the ground from sunlight coming through the treetops a hundred feet above my head. I could not see very far through the forest undergrowth, but I listened and watched for any indication of game. A rustling from some movement in the bushes just off the trail up ahead caught my attention.

Suddenly, a giant black jaguar appeared in the trail. He looked at me, calmly flicking his tail back and forth. Great yellow eyes with black slits fixed me with a curious gaze, and I looked right back without wavering. Both of us remained motionless, held by the force from each other's eyes. Time seemed to stop, and all of the usual sounds of the forest faded away from the suspense of our encounter.

Cats, even the big ones, do not like to be looked straight in the eye. This one blinked and turned his head away. Then with a low rumble in his throat and one effortless spring from his sitting position, he disappeared silently back into the undergrowth from which he had come.

As if waking from a dream, I suddenly felt my heart pounding. The shotgun hung in my hand, unused. I took a step forward, then turned and ran back to Jose, who was still tapping rubber trees along the trail.

In a gush of words I tried to relate what I had just seen. Then we both went to see if there remained any sign of my strange encounter. We examined the giant pug marks, as big as a man's hand, left in the soft earth by the cat's paws. Of course, there was no sign that the cat had been black, but there was plenty to show that he had been big. Then Jose broke out in a sweat and began to tremble, but I remained calm. "Weren't you afraid, Manuel?" he asked me.

"There was no time to be afraid," I replied. "Besides, he didn't seem to wish me any harm. He just turned his head and disappeared."

"A good thing you didn't shoot him with the bird shot in your shotgun. That would only have made him mad and brought him on top of you. You're a lucky guy this morning, Manuel," Jose told me.

Back at camp everyone got excited, and the story grew with the telling. No one had seen jaguars in the area, let alone the rare black one. They all wondered why I had not turned and run in panic. Instinct had kept me from making that fatal mistake. We all talked about it for a long time around the camp fire that night, and I was very watchful when I went into the forest after that. The black jaguar did not make another appearance.

At the camp, rubber balls accumulated as the men worked, and our supplies diminished from daily use. Soon it was almost time to return to the trading post at Iberia down on the main river. As I worked, I did not forget about my encounter with the black jaguar in the forest. As a matter of fact, the animal often appeared in my dreams, but he did not seem a menace to me there, either. I began to have the feeling that somehow the incident had some importance for my future that I did not yet understand.

Several months later we returned upriver in a canoe heavily laden with supplies and rubber cutters. We brought the same canoe back to Iberia loaded with large balls of smoked rubber. Mariana and Lino Vela organized a celebration for our safe return. A successful trip to the rubber-gathering area of our camp meant good profit for the trading post.

Both Mariana and Lino were pleased with Roque's report of my good progress in learning the details of rubber camp operation in the forest. Roque's report of my encounter with the black jaguar also impressed them. It indicated to them that I could take care of myself in the jungle.

After the celebrations at Iberia for our return, I went back to work with Lino at the trading post, and Mariana gave me the latest news from the rest of the family in Iquitos. Word came from Mother that I should be careful if I went into the forest with the rubber cutters.

The trading post at Iberia was a busy place, with visitors and customers arriving daily in the river traffic from the interior's rubber camps. Soon after I came back from my adventures upriver, I met an old man, a friend of Lino Vela's, named Julio Cardenas. Julio had recently returned overland through the forest from the southeast where he had been on the upper Jurua River. He said that *caucho* rubber trees grew in great abundance there. According to him, a man could produce more than twice as much caucho rubber in a day there than the men were making from *hebe* rubber trees at our camps. As this kind of talk went on, Lino began to make plans to take advantage of the chance to double his rubber production by sending men to the Jurua River. It sounded like more adventure to me, and I put myself right into the middle of the talk and the plans.

It didn't take long for Lino to decide to have Roque pick three men and me to get together an outfit for the trip to Jurua caucho country. Old Julio told us how to go an easier way by canoe rather than overland the way he had come. He said, "Take the canal from Iberia to the Tapiche River, then up a branch, the Blanco River, to its headwaters. Then there's a short portage overland to the Javari River. Go up the Javari to the headwaters and take a short portage overland to the Ipixuna River. This will take you to the Jurua. Go up the Jurua to caucho country." Julio told us how to find all the landmarks to follow on the long jungle trek. We all hoped the trip would make us rich from the caucho that Julio assured us we would find.

Lino knew from Julio that the trading firm downriver in Manaus, Brazil that sent him supplies, also had a trading post on the Jurua River. We could get the supplies we needed at this Jurua trading post and turn in our rubber production at the same place for Lino's credit in Manaus. It all sounded like a great plan. To me it seemed like the beginning of a big adventure.

Roque had chosen three good men to go with us to cut caucho, all skilled men of the forest. Traveling by canoe up the small back-country streams and over two portages to reach the Jurua River, I felt at times that a strange force pulled me toward some mysterious, unknown but important place. I said nothing of this to my companions, since I could not explain it.

By the time the five of us reached the trading post on the Jurua River two months after our departure from Iberia, word had already come upriver from Manaus to expect us. The trader outfitted us with the supplies we needed for several months in the jungle. He said that he would be glad to receive our caucho rubber and credit its value to Lino Vela's account in Manaus. When he heard, however, that we intended to work at the headwaters of the Jurua in Peru he warned us, "Be careful. That is bad Indian country. The Indians up there have been mistreated by the rubber cutters and now attack rubber camps that are not well protected by armed guards."

Roque seemed content as we went upriver from the trading post. He found that old Julio at Iberia had described the Jurua country well. Beyond the last rubber camps in Brazil, we began to recognize the landmarks that Julio had described. Soon we came to the small creek where Julio had told us the best caucho forest grew. There we paddled up the creek away from the main river and made camp.

Traveling the back-country streams and over the portages on the way from Iberia in Peru to the Jurua River in Brazil, I had a chance to learn more about the jungle. Roque taught me how to care for and use the Winchester repeating rifle. At our camps along the streams he took me into the forest to hunt for game we needed for food. That's how I learned the ways of the small forest deer, the wild pig, and the tapir. I soon learned to recognize the signs of the game birds like the jungle partridge, the trumpet bird, and the black jungle turkey called the *mutum*. At the various rubber camps we visited on the way, I picked up jungle lore from the night talks around the camp fires. Talk of life in the jungle was the main form of entertainment. By the time my friends and I reached our campsite on the small creek upstream from the Jurua River, I felt at home in the forest.

It took us several days using axes and machetes to open up a small clearing to let in the sunlight. We gathered poles and palm leaves from the clearing to make our shelters. A pole framework tied together with vines held up a thatched roof of palm leaves. Two shacks were all we needed. The larger one had a storage area in the back for our supplies and space in front for our sleeping hammocks. A smaller shed served as a cook shack. The shacks were beside a small clear stream where we tied up our canoe at the stream bank.

We soon found caucho trees scattered in the forest nearby, and I learned the way of making caucho rubber. The process was quite different from what I had learned of making smoked rubber from the hebe trees at our other camp. The hebe is a medium-sized tree and its crown mixes in the general forest canopy, but the caucho tree is one of the forest giants whose treetop stands above the rest of the forest. Its huge trunk has buttresses that give the tree support in the wind, and the roots, as big as a man's leg at the trunk, snake from the buttresses along the top of the ground and through the forest.

Because of the size of the caucho tree and the high buttresses, it is not practical to slash the trunk as is done with hebe tree latex production. Instead, the men cut the caucho tree down and then extract the latex from the whole tree at once. They cut rings in the bark around the trunk, limbs, and roots at five-foot intervals after the tree is cut down. The latex drips from these cuts into leaf-lined holes dug in the ground in advance. All this has to be done on the same day the tree is felled so that the latex in the bark does not dry up. When the moisture has seeped out of the latex through the leaves, the latex dries into large chunks of rubber. Several days later, we gathered up the chunks and carried them back to camp. Roque explained carefully and showed me every step in the process. I paid close attention to each detail to learn this new method.

We became excited about our good fortune as soon as we had time to examine the forest around our camp. Julio had told us the truth: caucho trees were abundant and game plentiful. Within a few days Roque set up a routine of leaving one man in camp to cook and guard while the others went out in pairs to cut caucho. Each man took his turn at camp duty, and each had an equal share in the production of the caucho rubber. For me, it was all a great adventure.

2

Indians

My Life Changes

IT WAS SOON my day to stay in camp to cook and do camp chores. Roque told me to prepare our big meal of the day and have it ready late in the afternoon when they would return from the forest tired and hungry.

As the men were getting ready to leave camp, Roque shook his head and said, "You know, I heard sounds last night that I don't understand coming from the jungle. We've seen toucans in the trees around camp several times since we came here. But have any of you ever heard that bird call at night? They never do that, but last night I heard toucans. And that jungle rat, the *agouti,* just like the toucan, sleeps at night and keeps quiet. But last night I heard an agouti chattering and squealing off there in the bushes. I was not dreaming, either."

Rogue continued, "Well you guys, we've got to cut caucho if we want to keep Lino happy back at the trading post and if we want to eat. Manuel, make us a big stew out of that deer meat I brought in yesterday, all right? And don't leave camp until we get back. Come on, you smart jungle *caucheros,* let's go."

The men took off on a faint trail and soon were out of sight and hearing. I spent the day cutting firewood, cleaning my rifle and shotgun, and sharpening the tools left in camp. Then I started cooking the stew and salted down the rest of the deer meat to preserve it for later.

Late in the afternoon, near sundown, the haunting, sad call of a nearby *tinamou* (jungle partridge) floated on the still air. Faintly, there came an answer from so far off in the depths of the jungle that it seemed to drift away. The men had not returned. A feeling that something had gone wrong kept going through my mind as I tended the fragrant stew bubbling away in the big iron pot over the open fire. I had expected my companions to return by mid-afternoon, wild with hunger. The times that I had gone out with them to work in the forest we had always returned to camp early in the afternoon.

Adding another stick of wood to the fire, I thought again of the warning about Indians we heard at the trading post. My companions had scoffed at the words of danger. "Easy-going Brazilian *seringeiros* (rubber cutters) might be afraid of Indians, but not tough Peruvian *caucheros*," Roque had said.

Now in the fading light of the setting sun, a noisy flock of parrots flew over in pairs on their way to a roosting tree. A sundown cicada set up a loud buzzing on the trunk of a nearby tree. The brief twilight of the tropics quickly faded into the dark of night. I tried to piece together the plans for the day that my companions had talked about before they left that morning. Two of them had planned to fell and tap a caucho tree already located some distance from camp. The others, I thought, were going to look for trees farther away. Perhaps they would still come in, but more likely now they would sleep in the forest. I knew they did not like to travel in this trackless jungle after dark.

I decided not to wait for them any longer. I ate my share of the stew and watched the flickering shadows cast by the fire in our small forest clearing. Night sounds were replacing those of the day. A raucous tree frog started a loud croaking up in the crotch of a nearby tree and was soon answered by another farther away. Two *tahuayos* (tropical whippoorwills) carried on a tuneful exchange of songs in the forest nearby. Once I thought I heard someone approaching, but no one appeared. The fire died down, and I covered it with dirt and ashes to hold it over until morning.

Disturbed and uneasy, I lay down in my hammock, but sleep would not come. The familiar sound of crickets and other insects made a continuous pulsing background hum for other irregular sounds of the night. A tinamou nearby sang out with a clear flute-like call, and a trumpeter bird also floated his call on the heavy night air. The plaintive piping note of a night monkey drifted down from the tree-tops, repeated over and over, faster and faster. The trumpeter bird calls seemed to alternate from different directions around the camp. Other sounds that I could not identify, sounds I hadn't heard before, drifted on the night air from far and near. These made me nervous, and I felt for the rifle I had placed under my hammock for security. After all, this was the first time I had spent the night alone in the jungle, and it was more than a little bit scary.

On the long canoe trip and during the days since we had made camp here in the jungle, I had learned a lot from my four companions, but I was still very much a newcomer and my nerves were jumpy. It had rained late in the afternoon, and now a rotten branch of some big tree came crashing down nearby. I bolted upright in my hammock. Trying to calm myself, I thought, "That's the reason for our camp clearing—so none can fall on us." During the night, another tropical downpour with lightning and thunder passed over the camp. It left cool air behind in the camp, and I had to wrap myself in a blanket to doze off into a troubled sleep.

With the first light of dawn, a group of noisy toucans awakened me with their raucous calling from a nearby tree. Taking up the shotgun with the idea of getting one to roast for breakfast, I stepped into the forest. But the partridge that I had heard during the night made the mistake of showing himself first and was soon in my hands. As I turned to go back to the clearing, a sudden feeling of not being alone in the forest startled me and the hair on my neck bristled. I paused to look around. The tall trees were festooned with vines and lianas, some attached to the tree trunks, others hanging from the upper tree branches. Small trees and underbrush made it impossible to see very far, even though the undergrowth was not thick in this forest of big trees. I couldn't see or hear anything but the jungle and its sounds, so I went uneasily back to camp with the bird I had shot.

After stirring up the fire and preparing a spit for roasting the partridge, I picked up a bucket and went to the nearby creek for fresh water. The clear creek flowed slowly and by then the sun had risen and sent shafts of sunlight to the forest floor. A dragonfly hovered and darted in and out of the sunlight over the water. The silvery side of a big *sabalo* fish flashed in the depths of a pool, and I thought of trying to catch it later. As I dipped the pail into the stream, a slight sound and movement caught my attention.

I turned my head and found myself surrounded by a group of naked, silent Indians. They had fantastic designs painted in black on their brown bodies. Each held either a sharp lance or a bow with the arrow aimed at me. Everything remained in suspense for a moment without movement or sound. Then one of the Indians stepped forward and took the hunting knife from my belt and the bucket from my hand. Two others immediately tied my hands behind my back with a vine. It all happened so swiftly that I had no chance even to think of struggling. The advantage of surprise was on their side and the odds more than fifteen to one in their favor.

The Indians led me quickly back to camp. There two guarded me while the others took our camp apart. One of the men gave commands, and in a very short time everything useful had been arranged into small pack loads. The half-roasted partridge that had been cooking over the fire was cut into pieces that were passed around. Not

knowing when or if I might eat again, I forced myself to eat the small bit given to me as I watched the camp shelters go up in flames.

As I tried to understand what was happening to me, my mind churned and I searched for something I might do to help myself. At one moment it seemed to me that surely my companions would return and let go with a burst of rifle shots at these savages and set me free. But then I realized that I was seeing all of the rubber cutters' firearms being collected into pack loads, not just those that had been left in camp. Where were my friends? What had happened to them? Had these Indians kept them from returning to camp the day before? And what was going to happen to me? We had heard stories about cannibals in this area. Could I possibly escape?

I turned my head to look around at the Indians, and noticed that my guard watched every move I made, even the turning of my head. All of the men were naked, except for a band of fiber around the waist. They were not large people, but were well-built and muscular, and all their movements were smooth and purposeful.

Within minutes the Indians took up their packs and formed a single line. They placed me in the middle guarded by the men just in front and behind me. Our caucho camp lay a smoldering ruin when we stepped off through the forest.

As we left the campsite and for the next few hours, I tried to keep track of our direction of travel. With the morning sunlight coming over my left shoulder, the route had to be toward the southwest. There was no sign of a trail that I could see, but the pace was fast. The Indians glided through the forest without effort, while vines and thorns constantly pulled at me. With my hands tied, I could not use them to help me balance. But from the first moment of the confrontation, an instinct for survival guided me to show no sign of weakness or emotion.

We continued on in a southwesterly direction, up and down hills through rolling country. I tried to note the small streams we crossed, but soon lost track in the struggle to keep up. It was cool, but with the moist air and the effort to keep my place in line, I was constantly dripping with sweat.

As the pace of travel kept on without let up, I became less and less aware of the details of my surroundings. By mid-afternoon I had become so tired that I could hardly keep from stumbling, no matter how hard I tried.

We stopped at a small stream, and my hands were untied. The leader, by example and gesture, showed me that I should wash my face and rinse out my mouth. I was so thirsty that I started to gulp down the water, but they led me away from the stream and would not let me have more water. Portions of smoked meat were passed out. Mine was so dry that I could hardly swallow it, but I knew I must eat to survive and somehow I forced it down.

After only a short rest they tied my hands again, and we took off in the same direction as before. The few bites of food helped me, and I found some reserve strength to go on. As dusk deepened into darkness, the pace slowed somewhat to make it a little easier for me. My exhaustion was beginning to show, but the march lasted all night. We did not stop again until daylight.

This time when we halted, again beside a small stream, I carefully followed the gestured instructions, rinsing out my mouth and swallowing only a few sips of water, even though I had an almost overwhelming desire to just gulp the water down. They allowed me to bathe my body. I was covered with scratches from a thousand thorns, and my clothes were in tatters. After only a brief pause we all took off again at the forced pace of the day before. We went on this way for another day and night.

Two days and nights of this almost continuous forced march brought me to the point of near collapse. For the last few hours before dawn on the third day I barely staggered forward. With the first light we came up a small hill and stopped. Here my captors opened a well-hidden deposit of supplies, while I collapsed on the ground in an agony of fatigue. Even breathing seemed to take an effort almost beyond my power. I could only think in bits of jumbled thought, "How . . . why . . . where?"

They allowed me a few hours of tortured rest and fitful sleep. Then one of them prodded me awake to eat. I was given a small clay dish

of thick, sour, mushy liquid to drink. This I found refreshing and stimulating and began to feel as if I were coming painfully back to life.

Late in the afternoon, I noticed that two Indians arrived at our camp from the direction of the caucho camp. They reported to the leader with many gestures, and I decided that they were a rear guard left behind to check if anyone had followed. I knew that we could not have been pursued. Even if one or more of my companions had escaped and gone for help, it would have taken days to reach the nearest settlement. It seemed to me very unlikely that any of my companions had survived. The Indians must have been satisfied, for they rested on through the night but did not build a fire. Before dark, one of the guards rubbed crushed leaves from a small bush onto my scratches and cuts. He did this with no show of sympathy or feeling, but I soon felt relieved from itching and pain. The bleeding stopped.

As the sun went down, moisture from the dampness in the air began to gather on the leaves and dripped from the treetops in a constant patter. For protection against this cold dripping dew, the Indians built small individual palm-leaf shelters on stick frames. They were only large enough to sit in, and mine was circled by the others, leaving no avenue for escape. I spent the cold night in pain and misery. My whole body ached from struggling over so many miles through the forest, and I felt alone and helpless. My thoughts were mostly of the past and still came only in disconnected fragments. But what of the future? What was going to happen to me? From the Indian stories I had heard in the villages and camps on the way to the Jurua, my chances of survival seemed small. But how could I separate truth from fantasy?

At dawn my guard prodded me awake. The Indians carefully scattered every sign of our camp before setting out again. At the first stream we stopped for a bath. Then we walked on, still toward the southwest, but at an easier pace. The Indians seemed a little less tense now that they were so far from the area of the attack on our caucho camp.

I tried to watch the country we passed through for landmarks and to keep track of the days. The Jurua River had to be on the right, for we had crossed no big river. The route now took us up and down hills, over fallen tree trunks, through swamps and small streams. Compared to the grueling pace of the first two days, this part of the journey seemed mild. We stopped every night to rest, traveling only from dawn to dusk.

One day it rained steadily. Shrouded in white mist, the forest felt eerie and strange. The rain filtered down through the forest from treetops a hundred and fifty feet above the ground. The heavy air was completely loaded with moisture. Every twig and leaf gave up its load of raindrops if touched. On a day like this *caucheros* stayed in camp, mended clothes, ate, and talked. But the Indians kept right on with their march toward a destination unknown to me.

On the ninth day of travel by my best count, I noticed one of the Indians rejoining the single file march about midday with a small forest deer slung over his shoulder. Later another appeared with two game birds. There had been no hunting earlier on the trip. The feeling among the Indians that morning had seemed different as we started off. Faces were less severe, and some talk went on back and forth between them. The pace of travel definitely picked up again.

About mid-afternoon there appeared off to the left a momentary break in the forest: a big patch of blue sky. Soon after, the trail led us past what seemed to be a cultivated patch of yucca, and I thought that we must be coming to a village. What would the end of this journey bring for me? Why had these Indians not already killed me? I was still sure that they had done away with my companions.

The way now led up a long hill. Suddenly there sounded a loud squawking of macaws, and almost immediately we stepped into a village filled with naked Indians. Men, women, and children crowded around and pushed each other for a better view of us. The hubbub of chattering and pushing stopped abruptly when a thin, ancient, long-haired old man stepped calmly through the crowd. He came directly to where I stood, my hands still tied behind my back. The old man deliberately looked me over from head to foot.

In just the same manner I looked back at this very old man who had an oriental look to his face. A feathered headband held back the reddish-brown hair that fell to the middle of his back. A few long, yellowish whiskers on his upper lip and chin added to the oriental look. Unlike all the other Indians who were naked, the old man wore a simple sleeveless garment of coarse white cotton that came almost to his bony knees. This man had to be the village chief. Instinct told me not to move an eyelash or show any sign of emotion or fear.

Soon the noise started up again. Children squealed; men and women grimaced and shouted; the macaws resumed their loud squawking. The chief stepped close, carefully unbound my hands, and told the Indian who had been in charge of my capture to remove the tattered rags of clothing left on my body. More people joined the crowd until there must have been more than a hundred of them. A group of old women came up close to look me over, pinching my solid flesh and cackling to each other. But one of them showed a different mood. She came toward me with a heavy palm-wood club in her hand. She muttered and glared at me. All of a sudden with a wailing screech she brought up the club and came at me in a frenzy.

The old chief, still at my side, gave a sharp command. The leader of my captors grabbed the club from the old woman and knocked her to the ground with a crushing, killing blow. A gasping sigh went through the crowd as two Indians dragged the body away.

At another command from the chief, I was led behind the old man into the largest of the round palm-thatched houses of the village.

18

Strange Village

Where I Am Born Again

THE ROOFS OF the large round houses of the village came clear to the ground. Inside the chief's house it was dark and smoky. As my eyes adjusted to the dark interior, I could see that the house sheltered several families. The only source of light came from three cooking fires and a small door opening that gave room for only a single person to pass. Many things hung from the rafters and poles that supported the roof.

The chief motioned me to sit in a hammock. Then my captors gathered nearby with the chief and started a discussion that went on for hours, with people coming and going. Two or three old women with black palm clubs took up vigilant guard duty around my hammock. In the closed, dark confines of the house I became aware of a persistent, musky odor given off by the people around me.

Soon, at an order from the chief, a young girl brought a gourd bowl of thick semi-liquid and offered it to me to drink. I found it strongly fermented and distasteful from the first mouthful and spit it out, handing the full bowl back. The girl reported to the chief and soon came back with another bowl. This contained a similar liquid, but it had a sweet aroma of bananas. I drank it with relish and felt

refreshed. When I handed the empty bowl back to the girl, she smiled at me.

The next few weeks were a nightmare of confusion and hopelessness. Later, I could remember very little of those days. I concluded that my companions had all been killed just before my capture at the caucho camp. Even if any of them had survived, they would never be able to find me here at this isolated location. I remembered my mother's warning to be careful about the dangers of the jungle. I thought about my companions on the trip to the Jurua River and my family back in Iquitos and sank into a hopeless depression that lasted several days. Gradually, though, I began to adjust to the strange surroundings, and a feeling of determination replaced my depression. I decided that somehow I would find a way to shape events to my advantage.

The pattern of daily life in the village seemed to indicate no immediate threat to my life. I could not understand a single word of the constant chatter that went on around me. There was a continual commotion in the house, where some twenty men, women, and children lived. Two or three cooking fires always burned. Pet animals and birds captured from the forest and tamed by the Indians wandered in and out. Day differed little from night in the windowless shelter. At least twice a day someone took me outside for exercise, but I was always well guarded.

I could see that as the novelty of my presence wore off, the stares of curiosity and grimaces of disapproval diminished. Some of my confidence returned when the children of the village started showing me considerable secret friendly attention. Sometimes a child passing close would reach out and touch me and then laugh. I realized that if I were being regarded and spoken of with ill feeling by the adults, the children would have avoided me altogether.

A few incidents of the early weeks I remember. Several days after my arrival at the village, a group of men dragged in a woman who was gagged and completely bound hand and foot with vines. They brought her to the chief's section of the house where I was also kept. When the gag came off, the captive screamed and raged, writhing on the floor, straining at her bonds. The men went off and left her. The old women took over as directed by the chief.

During the first two days, the captive would break into a ranting rage, screaming and frothing at the mouth every time anyone approached, but when left alone she stayed quiet. Obviously, she was becoming weak from lack of food.

On the third day, one of the old women of the tribe came to look. She stood and watched for a long time as the captive writhed on the floor, trying to break her bonds. Finally the old one shook her head and muttered to herself. She went away but soon came back with a bundle of herbs and a wooden bowl filled with water. She chopped and crushed the herbs in the water until she had a green semi-liquid mass. Then she approached the bound woman who began to struggle. At this, the old woman took globs of the mixture and spattered them on the struggling, straining body of the captive until she was covered with the green film of shredded herbs. Gradually the struggling stopped and the old woman left her victim apparently asleep.

The next morning the same old woman came back and cut off all the captive's bonds. The woman gave no outburst of rage and didn't struggle. As if in a trance, she walked out of the house, held at the arm by the old woman. Later, others brought the captive back bathed and left her sitting unbound in a hammock. The next day she placidly went to work with the other women in the gardens—a slave, perhaps, but not ill treated.

I had heard about jungle medicine and wondered if something of this kind of treatment was in store for me. I began to find out some time later when they led me out of the house to a place where the tribe was assembled. The chief, dressed in his white tunic, stood in front of the silent crowd. He waited as I was led up to him. There

appeared to be no threat in the gathering, but my insides churned with an uncertainty that I was determined not to let show.

The chief started a melodious chant and took from an Indian standing near him some branches covered with leaves that gave off a fragrant smell. With these the old man brushed my body as he chanted. Then a bowl full of a fragrant liquid was brought. Another Indian carefully bathed me with this as the chief continued chanting. The ceremony lasted only a few minutes, and without any apparent reaction, the crowd broke up seemingly satisfied. In the days that followed I anticipated some reaction from the bath, but none appeared. I still did not understand the language, so the meaning of the ceremony remained a mystery until some time later when I saw the same ceremony used on a newborn child. It apparently was a kind of baptism.

A few days after my ceremonial bath, a formal attempt to communicate with me in words was begun. Up until this time, any attempt at communication had been by hand and body gestures. Now pointing to a nearby object or handing something to me, the chief would say a word and wait expectantly for my response. When I responded he would repeat the word if I hadn't gotten it right. This helped relieve the boredom of my limited existence.

The restrictions on my life were gradually removed, but members of the tribe watched over me very closely even at night, never leaving me completely unattended. As I learned new words, slowly a link of understanding began to develop.

Many weeks later I was again presented in solemn ceremony before the assembled tribe. The chief began a chant that I had not heard before. The others responded and started a shuffling kind of dance as they stood in one place. A response passed back and forth between the chief and his men in a long and involved exchange. In the end the chief took a branch of large leaves and carefully brushed the full length of my body from the four directions of the of the compass— east first, then from the west, north, and south.

After this they took me down to the nearby creek where I bathed daily. Here a special herbal bath had been prepared in a large pot over a fire. After I had bathed they gestured for me to sit down on the ground with my knees pulled up under my chin. A coarse hand-woven cotton cloth was then draped completely over my body and head. The suffocating atmosphere underneath the cloth brought back my old fears, the same ones I had suffered during my capture and arrival at the village. Was this a sacrifice ceremony? Would it be better to jump up, resist, and at least die fighting?

I tried to pray for guidance, but it had been such a long time since I had received some meager religious instruction back home in Iquitos that the words and thoughts would not come to mind. As time dragged on, my nerves tensed, awaiting—what? The near-suffocation and muscle cramps became almost unbearable.

Finally the chief's assistant withdrew the cover with a flourish, and a joyous shout went up from the onlookers. The men gathered around smiling and talking animatedly. From the words and gestures, I understood that I was now one of them. I still had no idea how I was expected to fit into this strange, primitive world, but it seemed clear that I was now accepted as a member of the tribe.

4

Dreaming Together

A New Way to Learn

TO ME, LIFE in the village with the Indians who, I found out later, called themselves the Huni Kui (Real People) seemed worlds away from what I had known at home in Iquitos. Living in the rubber camps with Roque and the other men had done little to prepare me for this way of life. Gradually I became accustomed to wearing no clothes and to eating the unsalted wild game from the jungle, wild fruit, and the few vegetables, such as corn, sweet potatoes, yucca, and bananas, that the women grew in their primitive gardens. And with the help of the chief they called Shumu, I learned more words of their strange language.

After I had been with the Huni Kui for about six months, it became evident that the chief had something new for me to learn. Restrictions on my activities and what I ate became very rigid under the watchful care of the old women who were my constant guardians. My diet changed from that of mixed fare of food brought in from the jungle to only the roasted white meat from the breast of the jungle partridge, roasted yucca, and a mushy liquid made from cooked bananas or sweet potatoes.

Every two or three days one of the women made me drink a different concoction of various herbs. These preparations tasted strange, and they had strong effects on my body. One made me vomit violently, purging my stomach. Another worked as a laxative, cleansing my intestines. Still another caused me to break out in a sweat and made my heart pound violently. They gave me special baths and rubbed my body with herbs. The result of all this made me feel wonderfully exhilarated, and I wondered what would come next.

This treatment went on for about ten days, and Chief Shumu supervised every step of it, showing concern that my reaction to each phase was favorable. Even the people who had come to take me for granted as part of the village now showed special interest in the result of my treatment.

Finally, one day they gave me no food at all, and I realized that the chief and a group of about ten other men also fasted. On the day of fasting, this special group occupied themselves with having their faces painted. The women who did this used a red paint made from the fruit of *achiote* to draw intricate designs on our faces. This gave us all a special feeling of togetherness as we admired each other's painted faces.

Late in the afternoon, perhaps an hour before sunset, these men, whom I now recognized as important members of the tribe, gathered in the chief's dwelling. With Shumu we all left the thatched house in single file and stepped slowly into the jungle. We walked in time to a soft rhythmical chant. Everyone left behind looked on silently. I knew from the preparations that something special was going to happen but could only wait and see what the outcome might be.

A faint trail led us down a forest-covered hillside through a stand of huge trees of different kinds and shapes. After walking for half an hour we came to a small clearing in the undergrowth, a jungle glade with a stream running through it.

Here the large fluted columns of the giant trees seemed even more imposing because the undergrowth had been cleared away. The place gave the feeling of a great vaulted cathedral. Shafts of sunlight lit isolated spots on the ground. At sunset the birds repeated briefly the strange cacophony of calls heard at sunrise. The plaintive flute-like call of a tinamou brought an answer from another farther away. In the distance the raucous cry of the jungle falcon echoed through the forest. And briefly, way off in the jungle, there rose the roar of a band of howler monkeys settling in for the night, huddled together in some giant tree crown.

The calm of sunset deepened in our secluded jungle glade. One of the Indians imitated bird calls, and from several directions in the depths of the forest came answers. The chief nodded, knowing that we were well guarded and need not fear any disturbance.

Everyone else knew what to expect and calmly made preparations. One man kindled a fire from a glowing coal brought in a small clay pot from the village. Low wooden stools with their legs set firmly in the ground formed a circle around the fire. Soft chanting went on from time to time, but I understood little of it. Soon the men took their places on the stools as directed by Chief Shumu; my place was beside him.

One of the Indians placed a large bundle of dried leaves next to the fire. Beginning a new chant, the chief, accompanied softly by the others, picked up the leaves and broke off several small bunches. The chanting quickened. Chief Shumu placed a bunch of leaves on the fire, and a thick white cloud of pungent smoke rose in the still jungle air. With a large scoop-shaped fan of bright feathers, the chief carried clouds of this fragrant smoke to each of us in the waiting group, taking special care to see that I became well enveloped in the incense. The chants and smoke seemed to create a hypnotic trance among us. The Indians made each movement with the greatest calm and deliberation.

Before the fragrant smoke had all drifted away, Chief Shumu brought each of us a small gourd cup of liquid to drink. Although I did not know it then, this liquid had been carefully prepared from a jungle vine. It, along with the soft melodious chants of the chief, brought all our minds together as one. Closing our eyes, we dozed off and seemed to dream together, the chief controlling the contents of our dreams with his chants.

If all this seems strange, remember that animals have the ability to act in unison. Sometimes in a big city a whole flock of pigeons will wheel and turn in flight at an instant all together, as if directed by a single mind. Or a school of small fish will dart and change directions in the water as if controlled by a single mind among them. A herd of stampeding cattle or buffalo will do the same. Humans, too, have this ability, but seldom use it.

I remembered and understood very little of this first session of dreaming together until much later. The dreams I do remember began with colored flowing forms of blue and green going through my mind. These changed into images of the jungle—a butterfly wing pattern or a spider web. The dreaming went on and the men, including me, saw together in our imagination the jungle animals and the trees and plants of the forest as Chief Shumu directed us with his chants. I had no idea how long this went on before we all slipped into a deep sleep that lasted until morning.

A shaft of bright sunlight coming through the treetops struck me in the face, and I awakened. Then I became aware of the loud familiar chorus of several jungle birds. The men around me realized that I was waking up, they encouraged me with words and gestures as I came back out of our dream world. We sat around talking for a time, the men commenting on our dreaming together and remarking on my reactions.

About midday we returned by the same trail back to the village. In some strange way I felt changed by the night of dreaming, very different from the way I had been when I had departed the afternoon before from the now familiar village of conical houses.

After this session of dreaming, I found that as the days passed I understood much more of what the people said in their language that had at first seemed to me only a jumble of strange sounds. Many months passed before I could speak well, but I soon understood almost everything said to me. Little by little I felt myself accepted as a part of this group of people who at first seemed so strange to me.

As the weeks and months went by, there were more dreaming sessions. Much later, I realized that the chief taught me the tribal secrets with these dreams as surely as he must have learned about them in his own youth from his chief. One of the most important occupations for the men was hunting, and these experiences with the forest animals also became a part of my education in the dreaming together sessions.

5

Preparation for Hunting

Secrets of a Successful Hunt

EARLY ONE EVENING as Chief Shumu and I sat at the fire in the center of his house, Zurikaya (Colored Bird) came in quietly and sat down. From the chief's manner, it seemed to me that the hunter had been expected. The conversation soon led to the subject of hunting, and Zuri told a long melancholy story of his bad luck on recent hunts.

Wild animals and birds from the forest provided at least half of the of the Huni Kui's food. In order for the men to obtain this source of food they had to be good hunters. Many of the forest animals were difficult to find and shoot with a bow and arrow. A hunter with bad luck in his hunting came to the chief for advice.

Zurikaya told the chief, "The last time I came upon the large band of wild pigs that usually range in my assigned hunting territory, I misjudged the distance and approached too near the head of the band. Their leader, an old sow, saw me and gave their signal of alarm before I could loose an arrow. The whole herd disappeared as if by magic. Now they seem to have abandoned my hunting ground. At least they no longer follow their usual feeding trails. They leave no tracks or trace of rooting in the ground.

"The other evening I called a tinamou. When it finally came, after much too long a time of calling back and forth, I shot it. What I found was a bird full of worms from an earlier wound. Nothing left, and I threw it away.

"The band of howler monkeys in my area manages to piss and crap on me from the treetops but somehow avoids my arrows. The forest deer sense my movements from afar and evade me by leaving confusing tracks. The fruit trees that produce the favorite food for the birds and animals this year seem to bear nothing but leaves where I hunt.

"My family is being fed by others. This brings me great shame and leaves me with obligations that I will never be able to pay off unless my luck changes."

When Zurikaya had finished, the chief said, "Come back tomorrow night and we will look at it again with the other hunters. Bring all your hunting gear with you."

Chief Shumu sent word by his old women to a small, select group of the best hunters in the village. They came to sit around his fire the next evening. The discussion about Zuri's hunting went on for half the night. He brought all of his hunting equipment. There were snares made of strong twine of various thicknesses, treated with beeswax; a large, shallow basket woven of palm fronds used to catch the small partridges that sleep together on the ground at night; several lances for night hunting; a large bow with a dozen arrows of various types; and finally a bamboo knife, which usually hung by a string around the hunter's neck.

These things were passed around the group and examined with minute care. The hunters criticized defects they found. The snares had not been properly treated with herb juice to eliminate the smell of man, hence no animal would approach them. The partridge basket used to catch birds was just a little too big to handle easily in the forest undergrowth. The lances had surely been affected by the *iux-*

ibo (evil spirits) and needed a ceremony to counteract the effect. The painted designs on the bow and arrows could be improved in many details to attract help from the forest spirits.

After the equipment had been examined, the men questioned Zuri about his preparations for the hunt: did he use herbal baths to bring good luck and to remove body odors, special diets for getting ready to hunt certain animals, and charms for finding favorite game animals?

Then came a detailed discussion of Zurikaya's recent hunting experiences and his failure to bag game. Finally, about midnight, it was agreed all around the fire that a session of dreaming together would provide the only real solution to Zuri's problem. Chief Shumu told the men to come back the next afternoon for his instructions. When they came, he told them exactly what diets and purges they should use in preparation for dreaming together.

After several days of following the chief's directions, late one afternoon the men began the face-painting ritual, and the slow march to the isolated meeting place in the forest. Chief Shumu led the way chanting, followed by Zurikaya, me, and the expert hunters.

By this time I understood much more of what went on around the fire and of what to expect from the ceremony. As before, we arrived through the forest of giant trees at the same jungle glade where preparations had already been made. It was about the time of sunset, and we saw the upper crowns of the trees illuminated in brilliant golden light. Only an occasional deflected shaft of this sunlight broke the gloom of the forest floor.

Again the four guards took their places at the edge of the clearing, withdrawn from the others. One of the remaining men kindled a small fire. Then the ancient and fragile chief, chanting an invocation to the spirits of the forest, placed dried leaves on the fire. With a crackling sound, a cloud of sweet-smelling smoke billowed up. As before, Shumu bathed each of the dreamers in the fragrant tranquility of the smoke with his large fan of feathers.

With a melodious chant, he then passed around full cups of the magic fluid and we all drank together, seating ourselves on the stools around the fire. Others joined in the chanting, giving a tremulous obligato to the chief's song. With eyes closed, we each began to see in our imagination a flow of vivid changing colors, which gave us a feeling pleasure and exhilaration.

My sense of the flow of time disappeared, and for the first time in my life I felt as if my spirit floated free from my body. The flow of colors began to dominate the scene, and the chanting intruded to take control of the progression of the dreams in the collective mind of our group. Colored forms and strange shapes appeared at first without identification to known objects, soon changing into recognizable things of the forest in unimaginable detail.

As I learned the lore of the tribe, I found out they venerated the snakes of the jungle. The hunters admired the stealth of these creatures in capturing their prey, and images of the snakes usually started off any session of dreaming together. Now, with a change in the chant from Chief Shumu, the giant boa appeared, slowly gliding through the forest. A bluish light intensified the intricate design of a scroll figure that seemed to float along the boa's spine. The bold pattern on the snake's skin glowed with intense and varied colors. To handle a boa and pass a finger over the outlines of the patterns on his skin brought hunters good luck. Other snakes followed the boa, each with its own chant from the chief. They included a large bushmaster, a fer-de-lance, and many more.

Chief Shumu's chanting then brought on a parade of birds. First came the hawks, considered by the Indians to be a source of forest knowledge. An enormous harpy eagle appeared in flight, darting through the jungle vegetation with lightning-quick maneuvers. Finally he alighted, spread his giant wings, displaying his creamy white breast and the striped underside of his wings and then, his jet-black back. Turning his head and raising his neck feathers into a magnificent

crest, the eagle flashed enormous, baleful yellow eyes at the dreamers, and snapped his hooked scimitar of a beak.

Next came the snake-eating hawk, the forest sentinel who gives a shrill far-carrying call of alarm when disturbed. This one landed on the ground, and with downspread wings demonstrated how he killed snakes. There followed a parade of birds that served as a source of

food to the tribe. Each one repeated the various calls that could identify it when the bird itself was unseen. With each one there also came some display of its favorite living space in the forest as a help to the hunter watching in the dream.

Now the animals of the forest, large and small, each paraded before the group of dreamers when its chant was sung. Again their calls sounded, and with each there appeared some important part of its preferred locale to indicate where a hunter might find it. The procession took all night. I found out later that not all of the display of the animals came from Chief Shumu. If one of the hunters among the dreamers had some special experience helpful to Zurikaya's problem, he could sing his chant and all the rest would see it in their dreams.

With the coming of daylight, birdsong and penetrating shafts of sunlight altered the gloom of the dark forest, and the dreamers began to awaken. The usual unfermented gruel in a gourd bowl was passed among us. Drinking it helped us come back to our everyday world. After exchanging impressions of the night with several of the hunters, the chief asked Zurikaya, "You saw the action, heard the calls, talked with the spirits of the forest. Can you dominate them now?"

Zuri replied, "Great Chief, Shumu Nawa, dominator of all the spirits, leader of the Huni Kui, my understanding is renewed and increased. The forest will now give me what I need."

The chief then turned to me. "You saw the dreams better this time. We will do it again soon, and your knowledge will grow."

Soon we were all on our way back to the village where an inquisitive group awaited the arrival of the dreamers. From the remarks and the glances, I could tell that they were pleased with the reports of my progress.

I found again that my understanding of the language and of the activities of the village improved rapidly after the second session of dreaming together. The role I was expected to play in this strange world began to unfold out of the pattern of incidents in the daily flow of tribal life.

In the principal house of the village, Chief Shumu had a section separated from the other families also living there. From the first day, I formed a part of that special enclave. As the days passed, it became obvious that I was neither a slave nor destined to be killed. Also, as my understanding and participation increased, it became clear that the chief controlled everything that involved me, including my diet.

Hunting Expedition

They Take Me Hunting

HUNTING CONDITIONS WERE especially good during the early part of the dry season, before preparations for planting the gardens began. In order not to kill all the game near the village, small hunting camps were set up at this time of year at a distance of several days' travel into the forest around the village.

Chief Shumu's knowledge of details about the forest in all directions from the village was beyond belief. This came from his own experience when he was younger and from information brought back to him daily by the hunters. They all reported on the territorial movements of several bands of wild pigs and monkeys. These bands were fairly easy to keep track of because of their group habits and organization. Chief Shumu also knew the location and time that all the fruit trees in the forest near and far from the village bore fruit. This made it possible for him to know where and when animals and birds less well organized than the pigs and monkeys could be found.

Shortly after the second session of dreaming together, Chief Shumu decided that I should take part in one of the hunting camps. This would let me make use of the experience from the dreaming sessions and increase my understanding of the forest.

The chief assigned Nishi, one of the older men of the tribe, to prepare me and my hunting gear for the hunting camp expedition. Everything—a bow and different kinds of arrows, a lance, and bamboo knife—had to be made especially for the newcomer's use. Nishi took me to the forest, taught me about gathering the materials we needed, and helped me make the weapons. This took many days. Then Nishi taught me how to use my bow and arrow for hunting. The villagers watched with obvious approval the eager way the I tried to learn and the rapid progress that I made.

The day before our departure to the hunting camp, Chief Shumu prepared the prehunt rituals for the six of us who made up the hunting party. These rituals were expected to assure success for the expedition. The chief concocted several potions for us to drink and to use as herbal baths. Finally our bodies were exposed to the smoke of several smudge fires, each one burning bits of the hair of the animal or the feathers of the bird we expected to hunt. On the last fire smoldered the feathers of the harpy eagle, the greatest hunter of the treetops. All this activity was carried out with ceremony and chants to the spirits of the animals and the forest to bring good luck to our expedition.

On the evening before our departure, a beautiful cloudless sky indicated dry weather in store for the journey that I expected would bring adventure. As darkness increased and the stars began to show, a group gathered outside in the village center to enjoy the pleasant evening coolness after the hot sunny day.

A silent shadow floated in the deepening dusk and landed on the bare branch of a dead tree close by. The excited cry of a *weno* (owl) went through the crowd. A chant started and everyone but the chief joined arms to dance. The animation increased as the chants changed to hilarious insult to the owl from the forest animals, transmitted to him by our singers.

"Weno, I was with *awa,* the tapir, yesterday. He said that he would

use your oversize beak to make a soup spoon to eat with. Whoo!
Whoo!"

"Whooter, the last time I talked with *tshasho,* the deer, he was
scraping the ground with his hoof. He said that he would save the
scrapings for you. Whoo! Whoo!"

"Silent-wings, *yungururu,* the tinamou, told me that your leg bone
would make a good whistle to imitate his call for a sleeping mate.
Whoo! Whoo!"

"Big-eyes, *hono,* the pig, said that he would teach you to root in
the ground for worms. Whoo! Whoo!"

To get revenge on the animals for their insults thrown at him by
the singers, the owl was expected to direct the hunter's arrows to a
vital part of the animals' bodies during the next hunt. The Indians
considered the appearance of an owl just before taking off on a hunt
the best possible sign of good luck. The songs and dance lasted until
the owl flew away. As the owl departed on silent wings, the revelers
sang him an invitation to return. Then they retired to their hammocks to spend the night.

At dawn the next morning the villagers assisted the six of us in
getting our gear ready. During the process, the hunters got plenty of
advice on how to conduct their hunting expedition. Chief Shumu
spent his time giving Nishi, my personal guide, last-minute instructions on the training of the new hunter. Before sunrise we set off single file in a southwesterly direction. No trail showed in the forest,
and we left little sign of our passage through the undergrowth.

Natakoa (Man of the Forest), one of the best hunters in the village, took the lead with Nishi bringing up the rear. I took my place
just in front of Nishi. The front man commanded the march, and
the only person allowed to comment on our progress was the one
who brought up the rear. Our line of hunters slipped silently through
the forest at a rapid but unforced pace. I concentrated my efforts
on seeing how the man in front of me made his way through the

tangled vegetation of vines and thorn bushes without getting hung up.

We traveled the whole day without change of pace or making more than momentary stops. The route led through upland country with no swamps. We crossed several small streams where I wanted to drink water, but my companions did not allow it. These Indians very seldom drank pure water, but used mashed fruit or vegetables mixed with the water they drank. On this trip they carried a fermented concentrate made from yucca root. When we stopped for the night and made camp, this would be added to the water to make a refreshing drink.

During this first day of our trek, I found myself in good physical condition and able to keep up with my companions without trouble. Before dusk we stopped near a small stream and got ready for the night. Our simple preparations consisted of merely finding places close together where each of us fixed up a small palm-leaf shelter to sit under to break the rain of dewdrops from the forest leaves above. We ate food brought from the village and made no fire.

By the time we were settled, the gloom of night deepened the darkness on the forest floor, and the night sounds of the jungle replaced those of day. Close by, a jungle partridge sounded its plaintive call and repeated it several times during the night. Tree frogs started an alternating dialogue back and forth, and various insects added their humming and buzzes. My companions discussed and identified all these sounds so that I could learn to identify them. Off and on, the exquisite fragrance of a flowering forest jasmine floated on the evening air, drifting with the gentle night breezes.

Before sleep settled on the group, they reviewed the events of the day in the most minute detail. The hunters spoke of animal signs such as tracks, droppings, chewed fruit, odors, and calls, as well as significant plants by the trail, like fruit trees and the state of their flowers or fruit as game food. I found from this discussion that I had missed most of these signs. The camp conversation gradually drifted into silence as sleep quieted our comments.

At dawn we were awakened abruptly by a band of howler monkeys singing to the first rays of morning sunlight striking the treetops. I awoke stiff and cold from sleeping in a sitting position without any body-cover. Ice-cold drops of dew falling from the trees stung our bodies as we left our shelters. Mist drifted through the forest canopy and filtered the light to a ghostly gray. We munched silently on smoked meat and then scattered the leaves of our small palm-leaf shelters. Carefully, we wiped out any other indications of our presence before putting on our packs and moving out.

The second day passed much the same as the first, but I was determined to improve my observations of the jungle signs along the route. At a small stream crossing, I noted a single three-toed track of a tapir, heard toucans feeding in a tree, and saw the small fruit they dropped on the ground. At another place I became aware of the pungent musky smell of wild pig before we came to the area where the pigs had been rooting up the earth for food.

Crossing a rocky ledge on a hilltop, we all heard a dry rattling sound. Our leader immediately veered off on another course and soon stopped. After taking off our packs, Nishi took me cautiously back to show me the source of the strange sound. There in the underbrush a giant bushmaster snake lay coiled around its nest, a conical hump of soil mixed with leaves. Nishi pointed out the fetid odor of the snake as a danger signal and told me that I would soon learn the smell of other dangerous snakes also. In camp that night, I had some comments about what I had seen on the trail, but from the remarks of the others it was evident that I had again missed most of the jungle signs and still had much to learn.

7

Hunting Camp

I Learn to Use Their Hunting Secrets

NEAR MIDDAY ON the third day's travel out from the village, we arrived at our chosen hunting ground and picked a location for our camp near a small stream. Here three of us, including Nishi and myself, started preparing the hunting camp. The other three went out in different directions to scout the game signs and hunting conditions.

With materials gathered from the nearby forest we constructed a palm-leaf roof on a vine and pole framework using four small trees located just right for the corners. By the time the scouts had returned at dusk, the shelter was ready, providing space for six small sleeping hammocks. We kindled a fire in the middle under a meat-smoking platform of interwoven green sticks.

The scouts brought back game: two partridges, a small forest deer, and a pair of monkeys. These we cleaned, placing the choice tidbits low over the fire for a fast roasting, our first camp meal. The rest of the meat we prepared for slow roasting and smoking on the platform.

That night, lying in my hammock, I heard in great detail about each hunter's success, in addition to a review of the hunting conditions noted in the area around camp.

Raci (Bird Hunter) spoke first. "Nearby I found many roosting places of partridges. I have located their droppings on the ground. We will have a full moon in a few nights, and I will spear them from below as they sleep. Over the next ridge there is a large tree with small fruit, almost ripe. The birds are just beginning to come. They start before the monkeys. The branches of the tree are just right for building shooting platforms, and there are plenty of vines that we can use to climb up to the branches.

"When it came time to start back to camp I had no game yet. Just as I turned on my way, a small ground-sleeping tinamou sent out his sad call close by, and an answer came from farther away. Do you know why their evening call is so sad? They don't like to sleep alone, and at sunset each one wanders around calling until an answer comes back; then the two move closer and closer together guided by the calls. That's how they find sleeping partners. When I answered the calls, I found that I was located between the birds. So I backed up between the buttresses of a big tree where I could see the ground for a good distance in front of me, and started calling the birds to me. You know that it is dangerous to call the tinamou without the protection of a big tree at your back—the jaguar sometimes comes in answer to the call! The tinamou is also his favorite food.

"One bird soon showed up nearby and I took a good shot. He fluttered his wings and kicked a few times, but was soon with me at the base of the tree. I broke his leg and put a long streak of his blood under each of my eyes to bring good luck. The other bird, for some reason, came slowly. My call didn't seem to please him, though it seemed to me to be the same as his. Finally, but very cautiously, turning back and forth, he came within range and soon had my arrow in his side. By then darkness approached, and I had to hurry to get back here during the last light."

Then Tshasho Anika (Deer Hunter), who had gone scouting in a different direction, spoke up. "As I went through the forest I watched for a place where my deer plant might grow. You know the little plant that has spotted leaves that look like the skin of a young deer fawn? After walking awhile I found some good ones with well-marked leaves. I dug up the best one and chose a piece of the swollen root to chew in my mouth. Then I felt good because I knew that either a deer would come to me, or I would find him.

"I walked around longer than I expected, and the root in my mouth began to dissolve. There was still no sign of a deer, even though I took care not to miss any tracks. Finally I came to a hillside where the wind of a storm had blown down a large tree. In the open space left by the fallen tree, young plants grew up with fresh green leaves. I stopped at the edge of this opening in the forest and saw the leaves of a young plant vibrating on the other side. I watched, listened, and smelled the air, but could detect no sign of the animal I knew must have been eating on the plant that still moved.

"Very carefully I moved toward the plant, which now stood motionless. When I got there I found that some of the leaves of the plant had been chewed, and on the soft ground beside it appeared a perfectly shaped deer track. The animal had sensed my presence and left before I could see it. There are, however, ways to make a deer come back if you know the secret. I very carefully worked my hand into the soft earth under the deer track without disturbing it, and lifted it whole out of the ground. Then I turned it over and placed it upside down in the hole where it had been. At the same time I spat out the chewed-up root of the deer plant on the ground where the deer had been. Then I returned to the place where I had entered the opening in the forest, being very careful not to disturb anything or make a sound.

"From there I could see the spot where I had turned the track upside down. I squatted down in a position from which I could shoot an arrow and waited. To break up the shape of my face that the deer might see, I placed a leafy twig into my mouth and almost closed my

47

eyes. The smallest sign will make a shy deer go away, but I knew this one was still hungry and would be back. He didn't come quickly. I had to be patient and say his name, "Tshasho, tshasho" over and over to myself. Finally I heard a very faint sneeze, and knew he was clearing his nose, trying to smell me. But I had rubbed myself with herbs before going out to hunt and knew that he couldn't find me by smell. From the sneeze, I knew that he was very close, and I got ready with an arrow on my bow string. In a moment, without making another sound or moving a leaf, my friend stood over his upside down track ready to take another bite of leaves. His side was toward me. All I had to do was pull my bow string back hard and release the arrow. It struck him just behind the shoulder. One jump, a few kicks and eye flutters, and it was over. I rubbed some of the blood on my bow for good luck. Then I tied the legs together with a vine, swung the deer over my shoulder, and came right back to camp to get here before darkness. I think we will find all the game in this place that we can carry back to the village. Tomorrow I am going after a band of wild pigs whose trail I saw today."

Natakoa then told how he had heard a band of monkeys moving through the treetops out of sight. By giving the call of a baby monkey that has fallen to the ground, he stopped them and brought the band down to his arrow range and shot two. One had fallen to the ground dead, but the other held on by his tail up in the tree. Natakoa had to go up a vine to bring this one down.

After the recital of hunting stories, the hunters listened to the strange sounds of the night jungle around our camp and explained to me where each one came from. I soon realized that the Indians had much better hearing than I did. Some of the sounds they described and imitated I could not hear. The same was also true of many of the smells coming from the forest. Some were so faint that I could not pick them up from the Indians' descriptions. Gradually the talk died down, and we drifted off to sleep, all except the one assigned to

tend the smoking fire and turn the meat on the smoke rack. In a hunting camp, sleep was never continuous because the men changed the fire watch every few hours. The man on guard day or night had to be aware of all the sights, sounds, and smells of the surrounding jungle and report them when the guard changed. Animal activity is often more intense at night than during daylight hours in the tropical forest.

Settling down for my first night's sleep in the hunting camp, I went over in my mind everything that had happened on the hunting expedition so far. I realized that I had learned more about the forest in these few days out with the Indians than during all of my previous experiences. I was also well aware that, by comparison, my knowledge of the forest and my ability to sense critical conditions fell far below that of my companions. I determined to change that.

Early the next morning I went off with Nishi and Tshasho to look for the band of pigs whose trail had been seen the day before. Two other hunters went to the tree with ripening fruit. There they would build covered hunting platforms up in the tree branches. These would make it easy to shoot the large birds and monkeys that would come to eat the fruit.

The three wild pig hunters went off through the forest undergrowth single file, with me in the middle. The rapid pace set by the others made me pay attention to keeping up, and I immediately found it difficult to move fast and still maintain awareness of what was happening around me in the forest. When we came to the place where Tshasho had found the pig tracks, we stopped to discuss what to do next. Before moving off in what seemed to me the opposite direction of that the pigs had taken, they told me more about our prey.

In hunting a large band of pigs, they explained, the timing of approach and understanding of the animals' signals usually determined how many pigs would be killed. They imitated and explained the two principal signals of the pigs. At a certain type of loud grunt from the band leader, the animals would break into a wild run and scatter in all directions. A loud clicking of the teeth and a high-pitched squeal signaled an immediate bristling attack on any moving object that was not part of the herd. To protect oneself in the hunt and obtain meat required anticipation and recognition of these signals.

As Tshasho led the trio off again through the forest at a killing pace, I found myself straining to the utmost to keep up. Just as I became exhausted, we came on fresh tracks and stopped to look, sniff the air, and discuss the signs. The odor of wild pig filled the air. Tracks and disturbance to the earth indicated the size of the band, what they were eating, and how fast and in what direction they were traveling. This time we set off at an angle to the direction in which the pigs were going. Soon, with no sign of anything unusual that I could detect, my companions stopped and came abreast of me with arrows set to their bowstrings. I readied my bow, and suddenly, following a loud grunt, there were wild pigs running around in all directions in utter confusion. I managed to shoot one arrow and string another when I realized that just as suddenly as the pigs had appeared, they had gone without another sound. I looked around, and my hunting companions were gone also.

Nearby I found my arrow sticking out of a dead pig. Soon Tshasho and Nishi came back, each with two pigs and blood daubed on each of their cheeks. They insisted that I do the same and rub some blood on my new bow as a good luck charm. The two Indians were pleased, and I was proud of my first kill with my new bow. Immediately we tied the feet of animals together with vines and slung the loads onto our backs. Along the trail back to camp we gutted the animals and scattered the signs in the forest just in case an enemy might happen by. At midday we were back in camp.

After a bath in the nearby creek and a light meal, we prepared the fresh meat for the smoking rack by cutting it into long thin strips. The one who had stayed in camp began preparing large carrying baskets for the trip back to the village. The other two hunters soon came back from building hunting blinds in the fruit tree. They brought with them two large turkey-like birds called curassows. During the exchange of their hunting experiences of the morning, the bird hunters said that several large flocks of birds had come to eat at the tree where they worked but had flown away when they found the men working up in the branches. We all agreed to hunt birds in the fruit tree the next day.

Tshasho told all about the wild pig chase. He also explained more about the feeding habits of these animals.

"A band of white-lipped pigs has an old sow for a leader," he said. "They fan out behind her, but no one goes in front of the old one. She leads them on a circuit around a territory that she knows. They come back in their travels to the same place about every two to three moon changes.

"If you can come up on the head of a band of pigs without them knowing it and kill the leader, the rest wander around as if lost until a new leader takes over and gives the signals. During that time of confusion you can kill many pigs. They don't know what to do.

"If you are lucky enough to take the leader of the band and know the secret, you will always have meat. What you do is cut off the head of the old sow and dig a deep hole in the ground. In the bottom of the hole you very carefully place the head facing the opposite direction the pigs were traveling. Then you tamp earth in around the head and fill the hole to make the ground look just as it was before. If you don't do it just right, the pigs will come back and dig the head up, and your time will be wasted.

"When you do just as I have told you and sing a good chant to the spirits of the forest, the band of pigs from which you have taken the leader will be led by a new leader to pass the location of the buried head as long as the band exists. To have the meat that you need, all you have to know is when the band of pigs will pass the place on the

circuit of their territory and be there ready. If you are quick, you can always kill two or three with a bow and arrow. But don't try to kill the leader again. That will spoil everything. The pigs will disband and scatter."

Tshasho ended his story as dusk fell on the forest. The call of a yungururu (partridge) sounded from the jungle nearby. This kind of partridge awakens and calls out at intervals during the night. The hauntingly plaintive call of several limpid notes seems to come from nowhere. It is almost impossible to tell the direction of the sound, but if you have scouted the area as Raci had and noted the signs, such as bird droppings on the ground, the hunt becomes simpler. Raci waited for a second call and then left camp in the opposite direction to that from which the call seemed to be coming. He carried a bird spear in his hand, and soon came back with a bird for the smoke rack.

As Raci told about finding the yungururu, a sound new to me came from the forest nearby and all talking stopped. The call was repeated several times before my companions commented. From the sound it seemed to me to be some kind of singing insect. And it seemed to come from a different direction each time. As near as it can be reproduced in letters it sounded like, *"Wyetee, wyetee tee."* The hunters told me that if the insect could be captured it made the best good luck hunting charm they knew. No one made a move for a long time, but talk began about where the sound seemed to be coming from. They told me that it took the greatest patience and care to find and capture the prize. They all listened as the call *"wyetee tee"* sounded from the forest nearby.

"I saw the bush he likes to live on over there," said Nishi, "but there are others down near the stream."

"He's not always on the bush he likes to eat," came a reminder from Raci. This further confused the search.

Finally, after discussing all the possibilities, two men slipped qui-

etly into the forest in opposite directions. Watching from the shelter, those of us who stayed behind could barely see the hunters as they silently moved with caution into the bushes. For a long time the call was not repeated. The slightest disturbance near the insect would shut him up, and this one must have been upset. After what seemed like half the night, at last *"tee tee wytee"* sounded again. No sign of the hunters came from the forest. Finally, after listening to many repeated calls, one hunter found the insect hanging on the underside of a leaf of his favorite bush. The good luck charm was soon carried into camp wrapped in a leaf and cupped carefully in the hands of his captor. The others began at once to make a small cage of woven twigs and fibers. Later, with a feeling of satisfaction, the camp settled down to sleep, having procured the greatest game-finding charm an Indian could have.

The next morning before sunrise, all the men except the camp-tender went to the fruit tree where the platforms had been prepared up in the treetops the day before. Just about sunrise, three men took positions in their treetop houses, while two of us stayed on the ground to gather the birds and monkeys that fell down when shot. My companion and I on the ground stayed alert for animals that might come to eat fallen fruit. These might include agoutis, wild pig, tapirs, land turtles, and others, possibly even a jaguar.

The action started soon after sunrise and lasted until late afternoon. The *caimito* tree's ripe fruit was the favorite food of the large game birds and many animals. The men in the treetops gave the first arrivals a chance to send out their calls of discovered fruit before sending them to the ground with arrows. For the two hunters on the ground, it was difficult to tell the bird calls from the Indian imitations. As a bird fell to the ground, the arrow was pulled out and tied to the end of a vine by which it was returned to the treetop to be used again.

This day produced enough birds to make a load for each of us to carry back to camp. My companions reminded me with glee that they had captured a *wyetee tee* the night before. They credited the day's good results to having this good luck charm in camp. It took until late into the night to prepare all the birds for the smoke rack.

The next day three men went to the fruit tree to hunt and three, including myself, stayed in camp. With so much game to smoke, we needed another smoke rack. By mid-afternoon two men came back from the fruit tree with a few choice birds and word that Raci had gone off to hunt when the action had slowed down too much for him.

After dark, Raci came in with two small animals and a very disturbed look on his face. He told the men in camp that at dusk he had heard the call of a lonesome partridge and had answered it while finding a good place to call and wait.

"We called back and forth for a long time, and the calls seemed to come from different directions. There may have been more than one bird, but I saw none. I cannot recall ever failing to bring my bird within shooting range. I might not always get him, but at least I see him.

"This time, after much calling, I saw nothing and started back for camp at dark with the feeling of something wrong. I'm not sure just what."

Nishi broke in, "We are not the only ones in this forest who know how to imitate bird calls. You should have remembered that and broken off calling sooner. You may have given an enemy a clue to our location."

Nishi's statement caused a stir in camp and tension ran through the group like an electric shock. Nishi took command.

"Prepare to break camp. At first daylight we will start back. Screen the smoking fires so they can't be seen. We will fill the carrying baskets in the morning from the smoke racks, but put in all the cured meat right now. The fresh meat will go on top in the morning."

The camp turned into a beehive of mumbling, scurrying men. As preparations were finished, we went to our sleeping hammocks, but it seemed that no one slept from the mumbling and whispering that went on among the hunters.

In the middle of the night everyone was awakened by a wailing echoing call from the forest that no one could identify. It was not repeated, but no one rested any more that night. We put out the fires with dirt, got the packs of meat ready, and took apart the shelters, scattering all the pieces.

At the first faint break in the darkness, we left the camp in pairs, going in different directions, with plans to meet later at an agreed-upon hilltop. We hoped to confuse any possible followers this way. I went with Nishi and met the others as planned after sunrise. Without comment we formed a single file and set out at a killing pace with only momentary stops to adjust our heavy backpacks. As darkness fell we stopped, exhausted. We each prepared a small sleeping shelter where we slept leaning against our packs. Before daybreak we broke camp and again separated for the start of our trek. Well after dark on the second day, we stumbled into the village. There Chief Shumu waited for us, having anticipated our trouble and early return. An immediate hubbub started as the chief sent out messages calling for the men in the more distant houses to come.

The women took off the packs of game and brought fruit drinks for the hunters. A discussion started among the gathering men and the chief told the hunters that they did well to start back at the first sign of danger as they had been instructed.

The events causing our early return were discussed and tension mounted among the listeners. Much of the talk was still beyond my understanding, but it seemed to me that Chief Shumu's comments were desinged to build up the tension and challenge the men. Finally, after they had all talked over everything, the chief decided to send a group back to the hunting camp with Raci to investigate. After this small group had gone, Chief Shumu told all the other men to take extra care in their hunting and watch for and report any sign of invasion of the village hunting territory.

Several days later, Raci and his group came back without finding anything, but the feeling persisted from inconclusive signs that the village territory was being visited by outsiders. The whole village was disturbed by this.

Meanwhile Chief Shumu and Nishi took great pains to review with me in infinite detail every significant incident of sound, sight, and smell during the recent hunt. They fixed in my mind what had been learned, increasing my knowledge of jungle lore. From these discussions and from my daily experience in the village, I became aware of how closely attuned these Indians were to the forest where they lived. Often at ground level in the jungle you could see no more than fifteen feet. Looking upward into the treetops, you might sometimes be able to see as far as a hundred feet, but seldom farther. With their acute sense of the surroundings, the Huni Kui could avoid most of the obstructions and make their way quickly through the dense undergrowth. They reacted instinctively to the faintest signals of sound and smell from the forest around them.

Most of the jungle animals had protective coloring or patterns of camouflage coloring that made it difficult to see them even close at hand. The Indians had great patience when it was required, and together with knowledge and instinct, they used it to capture game with the least possible amount of energy. Many of the best hunters seemed to know by some special sense just where to find the game they sought, or had developed some special method of drawing game to them. Knowing how to imitate and use signals that animals made to communicate with their own kind helped an astute hunter locate game and draw it into sighting range. Developing all these skills made it possible for a hunter to provide his family with food to supplement what the women produced in their gardens.

Hunting Stories

How I Learn Some of Their Hunting Lore

THE TRIBE'S HUNTING lore was passed down from father to son by demonstration in the forest, but hunting knowledge also circulated through the village by means of stories. Whenever a group of men gathered together with nothing in particular to do, the conversation soon turned to an exchange of hunting information, both recent and traditional. As my ability to understand and respond became evident, the men made an effort to include me in these exchanges.

Some of the favorite times for telling hunting stories were cold rainy nights when the men sat around the fire in the chief's house. Stories were also told on clear balmy nights of the dry season when the moon came out and the people would gather outside in the center of the village. On full moon nights the nightjar (nighthawk) would often repeat its melancholy call from a dead tree in the village clearing and then fly off into the night sky to catch insects. In Brazil this bird is called *mai da lua,* "mother of the moon." The Huni Kui called it *nawa kano.* Its soft, plaintive four-note call, given in the light of the full moon, produces a feeling of sadness in all those who hear the song. In the Indian village, this sound would bring people out to listen for the repeated calls that nearly always came before the bird flew

away. The people gathered to listen, then lingered on to watch the moon rise higher and higher in the clear night sky. As they sat talking quietly, some chance remark would remind one of them of an interesting incident, and a long evening of storytelling would begin.

The Indians could usually tell from which dead tree in the village clearing the mother-of-the-moon was calling. Then they would watch to see in which direction it flew on leaving. It was their belief that good hunting the next day would be in that direction.

One moonlit night the people were out listening when nawa kano flew toward the hunting territory of Awawa Zuko (Toucan Hunter). He took his name from the largest toucan, which he hunted for its bright feathers. The night bird's departure brought remarks from Awa about hunting howler monkeys.

"Maybe the hunting off that way will be good tomorrow," Awa said, "but out that way today I did not get any great reward for my effort. There is a big fruit tree that I have been watching. It's in the territory of a large band of howler monkeys, and the last time I went by the tree, a few days ago, I found green fruit on the ground, picked and dropped by the monkeys. When I got there today I could hear the monkeys coming way off in the forest. From the direction of the sound and knowing their pathways through the treetops, I knew they would come to where I waited.

"There was not time to make a proper hunting blind up in the tree, but I went up to a crotch of the tree and broke off some leafy branches to hide myself as best I could. It seemed to take the howlers much too long to come to where I waited.

"As the band approached, still far out of sight, I could tell from their calls that something was troubling them. I heard the old males leading the pack give the sharp roaring barks that are their warning signals. When they came closer I could hear the leader making a deep, hoarse, clucking sound to signal his move ahead.

"They moved through a few trees and then gathered together. The leaders would give their warning barks and roars, then they would move on again. As they approached the fruit tree where I waited, I could see them through the treetops. From their actions I could tell that something on the ground had upset them. This made me very cautious, and I tried to improve my cover so I could not be seen from below.

"When they all gathered in a tree just a few feet away, I looked through a break in the foliage and I saw on the ground a young spotted jaguar, almost full-grown, prowling and looking up into the trees. He followed the monkeys, hoping that one of the young might fall to the ground. This often happens at a careless moment. But this time the monkeys had spotted their enemy and were protecting themselves with all the weapons they had.

"In addition to shouts and roars, they were breaking off dried limbs and dropping them on the cat. Also, I could see the monkeys deliberately pissing and crapping on the prowling animal on the ground. When they hit the mark, there came a furious snarling growl from below. This would be answered by a loud roar from the treetops.

"As the monkeys came nearer to my tree I could see that they were traveling with great caution, and this was why it took them so long to reach me. The fruit was ripe and when the first of the band entered my tree they gave the signal to start feeding. But they were very nervous and unsettled by what moved on the ground below.

"I knew that if I shot a monkey the jaguar would get it when it fell, so I just sat and watched. Beneath the big tree where I sat I could see a fairly large open area on the ground. The jaguar tried to stay under cover to avoid the junk thrown at him from the treetops, but I could tell where he hid. The treatment from above made him spitting mad.

"As I watched, I noticed the jaguar divert its attention to something on the ground out of my sight in the nearby bushes. In a

61

moment I saw a giant anteater, nearly as big as the jaguar, come ambling out of the underbrush. Immediately the jaguar, in his youthful frustration and ignorance, confronted the anteater, who calmly sat down on his tail and faced his challenger with open arms as if inviting an embrace.

"The jaguar circled with caution, and the anteater calmly turned in response. Finally, in anger, the big cat plunged with a roar into the embrace, grabbing the anteater by the throat. At the same moment the two great forearms of the anteater, fitted with tremendous claws for pulling apart ant- and termite- infested logs, closed on the jaguar. As the exposed neck of the anteater was ripped by the jaguar's great teeth, the backbone and ribs of the jaguar were pulled apart by the anteater's powerful claws. Both animals died almost instantly in each other's embrace.

"At the commotion on the ground, a tremendous roar broke out from the band of howlers in the trees. In the excitement of watching the battle below, I moved, and the branches hiding my presence fell away. The monkeys scattered before I could get off a shot at them.

"All that I obtained for my long wait were the claws and teeth of the dead jaguar, as we eat neither the meat of the jaguar nor the anteater. You don't often see that kind of battle. A grown jaguar will not attack an anteater. He respects claws superior to his own. On my way home I got a small partridge, my only game for the day."

Awa's story led Natakoa, my recent companion at the hunting camp, to speak up. "Several days ago I climbed up to a hunting blind I had made in a large fruit tree, hoping to get some birds. My son waited on the ground below. Before any birds came, I heard the clucking of a howler leading his band of monkeys to the tree where I waited. Howler monkey is not my favorite meat, so I was disappointed. The monkeys permit no birds in a fruit tree while they are eating there.

"This tree was a tall one, and from my position I could see out over the forest. As the monkeys approached the tree, a giant harpy

eagle appeared, seemingly from nowhere. He swooped and darted in among the treetops as fast as lightning. Before the monkeys realized what had happened, the eagle had grabbed with his terrible yellow talons one of the largest monkeys of the group. The others let out a roar as they scattered in the tree branches.

"The eagle, laboring with his heavy burden, flew to the very top of a nearby giant *lupuna* tree. There he placed the dead monkey securely in a crotch of a branch and examined his prey carefully. Obviously he found it more than he could eat by himself. He sat there looking around, raising and lowering the impressive crest of feathers on his head and neck. Then he started calling across the treetops with that piercing whistle we sometimes imitate for an emergency call. In a short time two others of his kind came winging in over the forest to help the successful hunter eat his kill.

"The howlers had all disappeared, and with the eagles nearby, I knew nothing would come to our fruit tree. I went down a vine to the ground, and we departed to look for game somewhere else."

As Natakoa finished his story everyone turned in anticipation toward Chief Shumu. He gave a slight smile, and a sigh of pleasure went through the crowd in anticipation. They all knew the story that was coming, but I did not.

With deliberate calm the old chief started his story. "When I was a young man and lived with my people in the forest many days' travel off to the north, we had as chief a wise old man called Awawa Toto (Great Leader). He tried to teach me everything he knew about the forest, and I tried to learn.

"One day Toto said that we should go off in the forest for several days. He had a special band of howlers that he wanted to show me. We prepared our travel gear and smoked meat for the trip and departed from our village early one morning, traveling toward the place of the setting sun.

"While moving through the forest we did not talk, but when we stopped to rest or to observe something special, Toto would tell me about the howlers. On the way we saw several small bands of these monkeys. He then would call my attention to their actions and teach me to understand their signals. These I have taught you, as Natakoa and Awa have shown in their stories.

"The howlers are not as fast as some other monkeys, but they are better organized and smarter than the others. As you know, a small or medium-sized band is usually led by a small group of old males. A large band of fifty or more is rare, but when such a group does form it has a large powerful male as the leader with a group of other males under him.

"Toto was looking for a large band to show me how it worked. That wise old man knew the ways of the forest and could usually find whatever he wanted there. This time it took us several days, but finally one evening we heard a great roar rolling through the forest that could only come from the throat sounding-boxes of a large band of howler monkeys.

"We moved nearer and found their lodging tree before they had settled down for the night. Then we withdrew and prepared to wait until the next day. Toto told me that the last time he had seen this band of howlers they were led by a large white male. He told me that the white one was larger than the others, which were the usual brown or black color. Toto explained that the white one had first been seen several years before near our village as a young monkey with the band. The hunters had all been anxious to kill the strange white one and had persecuted the band until it broke up into small groups and disappeared, along with the white one. He told me that if you kill too many of a band of howlers they become wary and will all hide at the least disturbance. They will also change their feeding territory. But if you hunt them only occasionally, they will continue to provide food that is usually the easiest to find in the forest because of their howling at dawn and dusk.

"Only recently had Toto found again the range of the white howler and discovered that he now dominated a large band of his kind. Before dawn we returned to the tree we had located the night before and waited there for the sunrise. With the first bluish-green light of morning penetrating the depths of the forest where we waited, we could hear stirrings and grunts in the treetops above us. As the first rays of sunlight lit the tops of the trees, a loud coarse roar broke the silence, soon joined by what seemed like a thousand other voices. The roaring echoed through the forest.

"We very carefully maneuvered into position for a better look. In the bright rays of the morning sun, seated on the large branches of the tree, we saw assembled a host of brown and black howlers of all sizes. In their midst, but standing apart, posed the grayish-white one, half again as big as the others. All their eyes watched him. He would rise up on his hind feet, draw in a breath, and roar. The others then joined in, and the sound went rolling through the forest.

" 'White Ghost,' " whispered Toto.

"Several times they repeated the performance and then stopped. The white one made some hoarse, metallic clucking sounds deep in his throat and started off through the treetops, moving from the sleeping tree to their feeding area. The others began to follow. At this point I stood up to relieve cramped muscles. Toto pulled me back down, but not before there came a loud bark from the trees. I had been seen. One of the large black males then came down to investigate, grunting *'Who! who! who!'* at us. All the others stayed quiet. The white one had completely disappeared.

"We pulled back under cover and stayed quiet—hardly breathing. Soon a gurgling or crackling sound was followed by the clucking call to travel, and the band took off again through the treetops. We waited until they got to the feeding trees, which Toto recognized. While they were busy eating, we approached cautiously. Only the briefest glimpses of the white one came to us. Wary and cautious, he stayed in the densest foliage out of sight. We stayed with the band all day so that Toto could see from their movements what their present range would be. He described this to me, and we started for home.

"Not long after our trip to see the great white howler and his tribe, Awawa Toto died. Then I had to take his place in our village. A long time passed before I thought again about the white one. One day we were talking about hunting, and someone reminded me about the white ghost. We decided to see if he was still there, far off in the forest.

"I chose three men to go with me to try to find him. We went first to the area where I had seen him with Toto and searched for several days. One night I had a dream that showed me where to look, and we went there. In the evening at sunset we heard the roaring of a band of howlers, far away, and hurried after the sound. When we arrived, the band had gathered in a large tree to get ready for the night. There we saw the great white howler standing in the last rays of the setting sun. I had a sudden impulsive desire to have his white robe as a trophy. The range was too great for an effective shot, but I brought up my bow and let fly an arrow.

"He heard the twang of my bowstring during a chance moment of silence and whirled. The arrow just grazed him, and there came instant pandemonium. The white ghost disappeared into a dark mass of vines and leaves at the very top of a giant tree crown towering above the rest of the forest.

"We examined the ground below where he had been directing the chorus and found spots of blood. The forest was silent, the band of monkeys gone. Nothing had come out of the clump of vines where the white one had disappeared. We thought we heard a soft grunting. I decided to go up and investigate. It was a long hard climb and darkness deepened as I reached the lower part of the tree crown. I could see the dark mass of vines above, but there appeared no sign of life inside. I could see only one approach through the tree limbs that would hold my weight. Near the hiding place of my prize I saw a fork in the branches. As I reached for this to pull myself up, the head of a tree-climbing viper rose up with a hiss, its tongue flashing out. This, the most poisonous snake of the forest, blocked my way to the hiding place of the white ghost.

"I saw no other way to reach my prize, so there was nothing else to do but climb down.

"We slept under the tree and heard not a sound from the howlers during the night nor in the morning. At sunrise I went up the tree again. I approached the last fork in the branches with care. The snake was still there. I could do nothing to dislodge him while clinging to the vertical tree trunk. Again, retreat seemed my only choice. We stayed around the tree all day, but could sense no sign of our quarry. The band of howlers had disappeared without a sound. That night, asleep under the tree, I dreamt that it was all a fantasy.

"The next day we went sadly home, without the least sign of any howlers. All the way back to our village I wondered if Toto would have approved of my action.

"Many times while we stayed in that village we went back deep into the forest. But never again could we find any sign of the white ghost nor any of his brown and black people. Only in my dreams did the white ghost come, now and again, to send his great deep-throated roar echoing through the forest of my dreams."

As Chief Shumu finished his story, small murmurs of appreciation passed among his listeners. After a while the villagers drifted, a few at a time, back to their houses. Chief Shumu sat for a long time looking into the night sky, probably thinking of his youth, before he went back to his house.

Invasion

Shooting Demonstration and Repulsion of Invaders

SOMETIMES DURING GOOD weather a group of men and boys gathered during the afternoon in an open area at one side of the village. The boys used this time for target practice with their bows and arrows and to play games. The men watched, commented, and sometimes participated in the target practice. A small bow was a boy's first toy, and he learned to shoot an arrow almost as soon as he could walk.

In one of the games, ten or so boys formed two lines facing each other, about a hundred feet apart. From this position they shot arrows back and forth at one another in opposing pairs. This game trained them in quick action and good coordination. Success lay in picking an arrow out of the air as it went by. To let one go by without catching it brought unfavorable comment from the men watching. To be hit by an arrow brought howling insults from every onlooker. Sometimes the men would play this game with hunting arrows—a dangerous pastime that frequently drew blood.

At target practice, the men demonstrated their unusual skill and coached the boys. Hitting a small target at unbelievable distances, then splitting the lodged arrow with another one, or shooting down an arrow in flight were common demonstrations by the good shots

69

and the goal toward which the other, less skillful marksmen worked.

On a day shortly after the interrupted hunting expedition, the men were watching one of the shooting displays. The chief came out and handed me one of the rifles from our destroyed caucho camp. This was the first time since my capture that I had seen any of our equipment. The chief must have noticed the shock on my face. To divert my attention, he pointed at the shooting target attached to a tree trunk and gestured to me that I should shoot at it. I tested the action of the Winchester repeater and found a shell in the chamber. With the breach open I looked to be sure that a dauber wasp had not plugged the barrel with a mud nest. I found the barrel free. Apparently the gun had been kept with great care. No rust showed on the metal, but the smell of smoke was strong.

I levered a shell into the chamber and raised the rifle to my shoulder. All target practice had stopped, and everyone in the crowd turned in my direction. During the trip from Iberia to the caucho camp I had been proud of my marksmanship, but now.... The rifle felt easy in my hands. I raised the barrel straight up and came down on the target, a small feather fastened to a distant tree trunk. Domingo, the cauchero, had taught me this trick for accurate shooting. Now on target I eased down on the trigger with a steady pull. The loud report exploded in the Indians' unaccustomed ears, and they all jumped. The feather flew into a puff of tiny bits and pieces of bark flew in all directions.

The sound proved too much for some of the onlookers, especially the children, who ran screaming toward the houses. But they stopped halfway, looked back, and hesitantly returned. Some of the men went to look where the target had disappeared. Others wanted to touch the gun, which I had handed back to the chief.

At this point a pair of squawking blue and red macaws flew over, up in the air a hundred feet or so. One of the hunters pulled back and let fly with an arrow. There came a gasp from the crowd as a whirling bird spiraled to the ground. A few minutes later I noticed

a hawk come soaring in over the jungle. It picked up a hot-air current rising from the sun-heated clearing of our village and went in a turning circle away from where we stood, but soon circled back around to take another turn in the rising hot air. The chief saw me watching the hawk and handed the rifle back to me. As the hawk came swinging back at an impossible range for a bow and arrow, I raised the rifle. I led the bird a little to make up for the speed of flight, and eased down on the trigger. The hawk exploded in a cloud of feathers and the watchers went wild with excitement. From my display of marksmanship, all the men wanted to look at the gun and touch it.

A few days after the hawk shooting, returning hunters reported to the chief that they had found unmistakable signs that outsiders had invaded the village hunting territory. This caused a great change in the tribe's mood. The women didn't want to go to work in the gardens that were at a distance from the village, where crops of corn, yucca, sweet potatoes, and peanuts needed attention. The scared children kept quiet and moped around without purpose. The men's hunting was unsuccessful.

This situation called for drastic action. The chief sent out several small scouting parties to find the source of the invasion. He told one of the groups where he thought they would find our enemies.

In a few days the searchers came back with their report, and the village went into a frenzy. A small camp of only two houses had been located three days' travel from the village, just where Chief Shumu had said they would find it. The chief sent another group to spy on  the invaders and check on their daily movements. The other men were called into a series of meetings where each head of a family was reminded of past losses to his family by attacks from outside. Chief Shumu reminded each one of his responsibility to avenge both the family and tribal honor. Plenty of opportunity came for the men to boast of all the great and terrible things they would do to the enemy.

Tension and pressure built up. By the time the second scouting party came back, the tension was nearing the violent stage.

After receiving a detailed report on the enemy's daily routine, the chief began to plan for the raid to eliminate them. The invaders were only a small party of eight, including men, women, and children, but they undoubtedly were backed up by a larger group farther away. Any sign of weakness now on the part of Chief Shumu's people would surely lead to a bigger invasion.

The chief picked fifteen of his best men—including me—to act as the raiding party. Then he chose ten more to make up a vanguard and rear guard for our protection. The serious preparations and consultations then started. All the fighting equipment passed under the inspection of Chief Shumu, and any defect was corrected. The weapons included two Winchester repeating rifles from the caucho camp raid. I inspected these for my own use. One of them was to be carried by my personal bodyguard.

An important part of the preparation was the painting of black decorations on the men's bodies. The juice of the *huito* tree was used for this. When applied to the skin, it produced a blue-black stain that lasted for several weeks. The various designs consisted of different combinations of wavy, jagged, or broken lines and spots arranged in unusual patterns. The women applied the body paint. The face paint gave an awesome appearance when seen at close range, but from a distance hid the lines of the face.

During the preparations, the men worked themselves into a fighting frenzy, talking about and demonstrating just how they would destroy the enemy. The displays of individual mock violence and aggressive action were awesome. Late in the afternoon when the chief could hold them no longer, we prepared to depart. Chief Shumu told of a place for us to gather, several hours' walk into the forest. We left the village by twos and threes in different directions to confuse any possible observers.

Later we gathered in the depths of the jungle, after much imitation bird calling back and forth. Here we waited for dawn and then very cautiously set out. During our stop for the night, I had time to think and wonder why I had been thrown into the middle of the conflict between different groups of Indians. It was clear that the Huni Kui (which now included me) must defend their home territory if they wanted to live in peace.

The next morning the leaders revealed their plan for our protection. They put me with two guards and carriers in the center. Out on the right and left walked protective flankers, with a vanguard in front and a rear guard out behind. Each group had signals agreed upon beforehand made up of bird and animal calls. These they used only sparingly to eliminate confusion within our party and to avoid detection by any enemy.

During the first day of travel nothing happened, but late in the afternoon of the second day as we approached the area of the enemy camp, there came a loud, ringing shout from where our front guard should be—then complete silence. With even greater caution we moved in the direction of the noise. There we found the vanguard grouped around a body on the ground. An arrow pierced his chest, sticking out from the front. The front guard had come on this lone hunter from the enemy camp. Before they could silence him with an arrow he had given the shout we all had heard.

This caused us some anxiety since we did not know who else might have heard the call. After a long discussion we decided to move into position in the forest around the nearby enemy camp, and make ready for a predawn attack. Signals for the night and for the beginning of the attack were given, and then we all moved stealthily into position in the falling darkness.

As we waited for calls to interpret and tried to anticipate what might happen, the tension kept us all awake most of the night. I dozed off until a companion nudged me awake in the first blue-green light of dawn penetrating the forest.

The signal came to move to the edge of the clearing and await the final call for the attack: the hooting of an owl repeated in a certain rhythmic sequence. The call came a few minutes later and brought a wild shouting rush from the jungle into the small clearing. We found the camp empty, probably abandoned the evening before when the warning shout had come from the forest. The men picked up the few artifacts left behind and set fire to the houses. Not a shot had been fired.

After a brief consultation we sent a group of men to examine the forest nearby for signs of the inhabitants. When nothing was found we agreed to meet at a known point in the forest in the afternoon on the way home. Then we broke up into small groups to make our way separately to the meeting place. With the raid on our enemies accomplished, the main reason for extreme caution no longer existed, and the return home was more relaxed than the trip out. I soon learned, however, that in the forest one must never be off guard.

The following morning a shower of arrows came through the trees as our party broke camp after passing the night in the forest. No one could be seen in the forest undergrowth. The arrows must have been aimed at a sound, not a sighted target. No one was hit, but a shout went up. I had a rifle in my hands and emptied the shell magazine in a rapid fire of shots in the direction from which the arrows had come. We sent a party in search of the attackers, but nothing could be found.

Late that afternoon, the chief met us when we entered the village. He came up to me, took my hand and raised it high, and said so everyone present could hear, "Were you not afraid, my son?" Everyone in the party assured the chief that of course I had not been afraid, and from that day on I was considered to be his son.

Then the chief gave orders to prepare for a victory celebration. It began later with a chant about battle and domination of our enemies, growing livelier as it progressed. Soon a snake dance formed with the men and women linking their arms together at the elbow and forming a long line. The dancers wove in and out among the houses of the village behind a leader with a feathered baton. The chants alternated between the leader and his followers. At a change in the chant, the women formed an inner circle with the men outside. Dancing continued in this way with the chants now alternating between the men and the women. Some of the dancers had bands of hollowed out seeds on their legs that acted as rattles, accentuating the rhythm of their stamping feet. This dancing continued through the night with only brief intervals of rest, until everyone was exhausted and the tension built up by the preparation for the raid had completely worn off.

10

Apprenticeship

How I Learn the Tribal Secrets

AFTER THE RAID, life in the village settled down again. The enemy invading the Huni Kui's territory had apparently withdrawn. The tension disappeared, and the women went back to work in their gardens. The men again took up organized hunting. The chief kept a close watch over all these activities, giving the necessary directions to keep things going according to his wishes and plans.

My position noticeably improved after I took part in the defense of the village and the chief addressed me as his son. My ability to shoot the rifle without flinching from the awesome noise of thunder when I pulled the trigger gave me special status among the Indians. To them the rifle was a strange and awesome thing. The hunters invited me to participate in their discussions of hunting conditions and experiences, and the old women that cooked at Chief Shumu's fire made it a point to see that I always got choice portions of the daily fare. My food was served to me by the young girl who brought me the first bowl of banana gruel the day I arrived. She often smiled at me, and we began to converse as I learned the language.

Gradually I began to feel more at home in the village scene, and the memory of my former life faded away. Soon I found that the

chief's program for my training was far from finished. Chief Shumu now prepared a series of combined herbal purges, baths, and a diet that had subtle effects on my feelings and bodily functions. Before my life among the Indians, I had heard the usual rumors about Indian medicine and witch doctor activities, and there had always been a certain fascination in this for me. Now, since I felt secure in my position in the village, I was determined to observe and learn all that I could, and I cooperated with the chief without hesitation.

After several days of preparation, during which Chief Shumu had supervised every detail, he and I began a series of sessions of dreaming together. For me this turned out to be an incredible experience, revealing unexpected things. Just within the edge of the forest that surrounded the village, the chief ordered that a small shelter be built. In it, there was only room to hang two hammocks with a small fire between. Outside the shelter a small cleared space also provided room for two hammocks to be hung between the trees. Here we were well guarded from intrusion of any kind. An old woman brought food on a signal from the chief. Village sounds did not reach this place of solitude.

Chief Shumu and I went to this secluded site alone one morning. On the way, as I followed the chief, I wondered how old he might be. Outwardly his physical features did not give the usual signs of age. His skin was not unusually wrinkled, nor did his flesh sag on his bones. Yet something about the man gave the impression of an ancient being. Reverence and admiration dominated the feelings of the tribe toward their headman. He maintained a calm, distant aloofness from the people and their activities, yet gave the feeling of complete awareness of present, past, and future events. I felt that the awe of the villagers toward their chief was justified.

Now Chief Shumu led the way toward the forest at his usual slow, deliberate walk, which added to my impression of his great age. He chose each step with care. On the way he started a low chant, seemingly to himself:

> Spirits of the forest
> bring us knowledge of the realm;
> assist in the guidance of our people;
> give us the stealth of the boa,
> the penetrating sight of the hawk and owl,
> the acute hearing of the deer,
> the brute endurance of the tapir,
> the grace and strength of the jaguar,
> and the knowledge and tranquility of the moon;
> kindred spirits, guide our way.

On this clear day of the early dry season, a few isolated cotton-puff clouds drifted in the azure sky as the two of us stepped from the village clearing into the mottled shade of the cool forest. Preparations had been made in advance, but no one was present. The old man gave a birdcall, and an answer came from somewhere out of sight. A tiny, newly kindled fire glowed in the center of the small opening in the undergrowth. Beside it lay a bunch of the leaves used to make the fragrant smoke. The small clearing revealed the massive trunk buttresses of the trees that supported the leafy roof of the forest a hundred feet above the ground. The tree trunks, draped with vines and hanging plants, were visible in the shade of the forest. Sometimes the shade was broken by brilliant rays of direct sunlight coming through the tree tops. Details otherwise unnoticed stood out momentarily in vivid clarity in these illuminating shafts of light.

At a motion from the chief, I sat down comfortably in a hammock hung low outside the shelter. Chanting, the old man deliberately put a bunch of leaves on the fire. Billowing clouds of fragrant smoke filled the still air.

> O most powerful spirit
> of the bush with the fragrant leaves,

we are here again to seek wisdom
give us tranquility and guidance
to understand the mysteries of the forest
and the knowledge of our ancestors.

We savored together the fragrant smoke that drifted around us
and up into the vaulted structure of the forest. Every immediate sound
and movement seemed suspended by the magic vapor. Before the
enchanted spell drifted away with the smoke, Chief Shumu poured
a cupful of the juice from the vine and chanted:

Phantom-revealing spirit of the vine
we seek your guidance now
help us understand
the past and the future
to improve our life;
reveal the secrets we need.

He came to my side and said, "You drink alone this time, but we
will dream together. I will be here to guide you. All is well. Your
preparations have been completed, every reaction favorable. Drink
it all and prepare. Pleasant and profound dreams will come to you.
With care we can direct the flow of the dreams. I will not leave your
side. This I have done times without number. When done this way
it will all come out well."

We reclined in our hammocks. My gaze drifted off up into the
tree tops above me. There I became aware of undreamt beauty in the
details of the leaves, stems, and branches. As my attention settled on
each leaf, it seemed to glow with a greenish golden light. A nearby
bird trilled and the irregular sequences of the *siete cantos* (seven songs)
floated down from above. Exquisite and shimmering, the song seemed
almost visible. The notes of the birdsong separated and were suspended in time so that each sound could be savored in its turn. A

breath of cool air drifted by from the forest, carrying sensations of pleasant aromas.

The chief spoke in a low, pleasant tone, "Dreams begin." With two words of magic he completely captured the attention of my mind. Instantly all barriers between us melted away. The mere glance of an eye or slightest change of expression on the old man's face carried his full meaning. We each knew the other's thoughts.

Chief Shumu said, "From the hunting camp we found there is much of the forest that you do not see and understand. We will now change that. You must have complete knowledge of the forest to assist the men in dreaming together ceremonies to improve their hunting. Thus we can all eat well and be content." A few simple words and slight gestures transmitted the full intent of his message.

The chief said, "We will start with dreams of the game birds. You must know everything about them—how they live together, make their nests, raise their young, and what food they eat. You must know the songs and other sounds they make—everything." Then in infinite detail the chief showed me, in my dreams, the life in the forest of the various tinamous (partridges), the trumpeter, the curassows, and other important game birds.

Then the chief said, "Remain with your eyes closed and let the dreams flow before we go on to other things of the forest."

The sense of time passing seemed to disappear for me. In my dreams, tracings of light and shade developed over a geometric pattern that moved in rhythm. Sometimes these forms resembled familiar patterns of spider webs or butterfly wings. With the sound of a birdcall or an insect buzz from the forest came a brilliant flash of color or rippling waves, depending on the character of the sound. These images gradually faded away, and the chief was aware of this change. When he spoke to me, I roused myself and realized that it was late afternoon.

Again Chief Shumu spoke, "We have night work to do. It will take another cup of juice from the magic vine. You will find the dreams now even more striking. Listen for my instructions and have no fear."

Then the chief built up the smoldering fire so there was a dancing flame in the gathering dusk. He handed the cup to me, and I drank its contents without hesitation. In the fading light I became aware of the acute ability to see details of the forest far beyond anything known to me before. The mighty trees surrounding us took on a deep spiritual quality of obedient goodness. As the fire died back to glowing coals, darkness settled over everything. In the darkness I could see what in other circumstances would have been completely invisible. I understood now how the Indians could travel with ease through the forest and even hunt at night.

A passing firefly lit up the scene with brilliance that seemed to approach the light of day. With sounds of the night coming from the forest, I also realized that my sense of hearing had become more acute. I could separate the night sounds from far and near and tell their source. The call of an owl, *Whooo whooo,* floated on the still night air, and there came an answer from off in the dark forest.

"You will learn to see and hear at night as clearly as the owl," commented the chief. And I felt that it was already true.

With chants and calls of the various animals, the chief brought into my dreams vivid episodes in the lives of night animals. Chief Shumu's chants, the calls, and the dreams they brought all became a part of my own learning. Morning sunlight breaking through forest tree tops awakened me from a strange sleep that I could not remember falling into. I felt as though I were coming back from a distant journey to unknown and unremembered places.

The chief helped me wake up by giving me a large bowl of finely ground fruit mush to drink. Soon the two of us walked at Chief Shumu's usual measured pace back into the village.

It turned out that this dreaming session alone with Shumu began a period of intensive training. Still on a strict diet and restricted activities, I had a dreaming session with the chief in the forest every eight days. There we examined plants and their various uses for food and medicine, as well as pursuing further study of the birds and other animals. During the time between these sessions someone often took me into the forest both at night and during the day. On these excursions I found to my satisfaction that the intensified sense perception gained in the dreaming sessions with the chief stayed with me. In the forest my companions pointed out the origins of each sound and smell, continually testing my progress in becoming completely at one with the forest environment.

After each series of four sessions with the chief eight days apart, Chief Shumu gave me an equivalent period to work with and understand the new experience and knowledge. Then a new series of dreaming sessions would begin. This went on for months. At times I became nervous and high-strung. I felt as if I might be going crazy. The chief and the old women noticed this. They took pains to explain and reassure me that as long as I followed the diets and instructions, everything would come out well.

I learned that the chief's old women were individuals who for one reason or another had lost all members of their family and thus had no means of support. They joined the chief and became important members of the tribe. Usually operating in the background they kept the chief informed of all that went on in the tribal activities that he might otherwise not know about. They gathered and prepared the herbs Chief Shumu needed for various uses and passed down to the young girls the techniques of making pottery and weaving cotton cloth. They assisted the chief in teaching me the things I needed to know about tribal life.

During the period of my intensive training I became aware of changes in how my mind worked. I could anticipate events and reactions of the people. I knew this was important in understanding how Chief Shumu guided the community in all of its activities.

As the training progressed, it became evident that the chief had a feeling of urgency to impart his fund of knowledge and experience to me. During the rest periods between dreaming sessions, in addition to my going out with the hunters I often was taken out by Chief Shumu on short excursions to the nearby forest. There the chief pointed out the plants that we had seen in the dreams and explained their use. He gave to me alone the secrets of medicine preparation and use and repeated the chants that should accompany both preparation and application. The Huni Kui strongly believed that the chants helped to bring about the desired effect of the treatment. In my eagerness to learn, I began to have a feeling of pride in holding the secrets that no one else but Chief Shumu possessed. The old man seemed satisfied that his obligation to pass on lore of his people was being fulfilled.

11

Indian Caucho

How I Gained Power Over My Future

ONE DAY SEVERAL weeks after the end of the dreaming sessions, the men were watching the boys shoot arrows at one another in the open area beside the village. Also, a group of youngsters were playing the game of batting a cornhusk ball back and forth, trying to keep the ball from touching the ground. Sometimes I entered this game with the Indian boys. Back in Iquitos I had helped organize a soccer team that beat all challengers. In the Indian village I took pleasure in teaching the boys how to kick the ball high in the air, and then as it came down butt it back up in the air with my head. This maneuver delighted the young Indians, and they soon learned the trick. Now as our ball game broke up, target practice with bows and arrows began.

It had been several months since the raid on the invaders, and since then firearms had not been seen or mentioned. Now Chief Shumu showed up and asked me to demonstrate shooting again, sending one of the men to get a rifle. With the first shot I demolished a small target on a distant tree trunk. Some of the men showed less fear of the rifle than before, and the chief encouraged one or two to handle it. This they did with a look of awe on their faces. Then Chief Shumu turned and asked me if the men could learn to shoot.

Now all eyes turned to see what I would say. No one breathed a sound. I felt that somehow a crucial turn of events awaited my reply. I answered, "Yes, but it will use up many bullets. We might need the ammunition to defend ourselves against the invaders if they come back."

The rifle changed hands carefully among the group without further comment. With dusk coming on everyone drifted back toward the houses. Chief Shumu walked at my side. After a few moments of silence he paused and turned toward me, asking, "Could you not get more guns and bullets for us?"

For a moment I felt that a bomb had burst in my head. I could not control my racing thoughts: get more guns, where, with what? I took care that none of this confusion showed on my face. After a brief pause, I answered calmly, "It depends on producing caucho rubber for trade."

Then the chief asked, "Can you not train the men to make caucho?"

I answered simply, "Yes, if they will follow my instructions."

Slowly the group moved toward the houses with no more talk. But my mind raced with the possible meaning of the exchange. Somehow I had the feeling that some power over future events might now come within my grasp. So far with the Huni Kui, I had just gone along with events, day by day, not thinking of the future or the past. Perhaps from now on I could influence what happened. There might be choices—dangers, too. But for a youth of fifteen, risks meant little.

During this exchange it seemed to me that I made the transition to manhood. No longer would I be kicking around the cornhusk ball with the boys of the village. The next day the chief brought the matter up again. "To produce caucho, tools are needed. What are they?"

"Good sharp axes and machetes," I answered.

"We have some, but the people do not know how to use them."

"Show them to me," I replied.

Chief Shumu ordered all the axes and machetes brought in to him.

The few axes they brought had the cutting edges worn down to the kind of blunt edge found on their stone axes. The machetes were mostly fragments, except for a few that probably came from the raid on the Jurua caucho camp where I had been captured. These the chief had kept unused.

I found a piece of sandstone suitable for grinding the tools. Then the chief ordered the men to grind the axes and machetes as I showed them. I also asked the hunters to locate the caucho trees in their hunting territories, so we could decide where the work would begin.

In a few days they had the equipment ready—axes, machetes, and several heavy wooden mallets made to my specifications. Meanwhile, the hunters had located many caucho trees in the forest around the village. The chief picked a group of men to learn how to cut caucho rubber.

Before my capture, I had worked with Roque on bleeding several caucho trees of their latex. From this I knew that my men were now in for some really hard work and I wondered how the Indians would take to it. Although I took care not to let it show, I felt excited about this new enterprise. It gave meaning and a new direction to my life, even though I could not yet foresee where it might lead.

In the beginning the work produced a big mess. Teaching the men the strange new tasks involved was complicated by the fact that the men alternated cutting rubber with days of hunting. Even the most willing of them could not be kept at that kind of hard work day after day. Also they had to support their families with their hunting. The men were eager to learn, however, especially when I told them of some of the things I would get for them with the rubber.

Before long we had a good rotating labor force. No labor shortage existed. Chief Shumu assigned the men to this work just as he appointed hunting areas and garden plots. It took many weeks to produce twenty blocks of rubber, each big enough for a one-man pack load, all together nearly a ton of rubber.

When the twenty blocks were ready, the chief began to pick men for the trip to the trading post. Any discussion about where the rubber would be traded, when I was present, gave little detail. I was unable to find out anything about how far away we had to go or in which direction. The chief made a careful selection of the men, choosing the strongest and most reliable ones. By this time I knew them fairly well from working in the forest with them producing the rubber, and I was pleased with the selection.

Each packer set about preparing his pack harness and pad. My equipment for the trip consisted of one of the rifles, a machete, and a small pack containing a rolled-up pair of pants and a shirt. These the chief dug up from his store of captured goods taken on raids of caucho camps. When I tried on the clothes the Indians looking on laughed and poked one another. I felt strange, but realized that clothes would be needed where I was going. The chief and I and both knew that I could not go naked into a rubber trading post.

After a few days of preparation we took off through the trackless forest, moving toward the northeast. I still had no idea of where we were going. I could tell by the talk that the Indians were heading for a specific location familiar to them.

For several days we traveled overland in the same general direction, without crossing any major streams. One day at mid-afternoon we came to a large river. My companions told me it was the Hono-Diri-Ra, the river with rapids. This information did not help me in locating my position. At the river's edge we stopped and made camp. Nishi, the leader, knew that blocks of rubber would float. While the others made camp, scouts were sent down along the riverbank. During the night they came back and reported the river clear of people. In the morning the blocks of rubber were strung together on a vine and tied between two small log rafts made from logs cut in the riverbank forest. The men worked eagerly at this task because it meant relief from the tedious packing of the heavy loads.

Hunters and scouts were sent out ahead before the flotilla started on its voyage down river. Long rafting poles used to push on the river bottom helped control the progress of the rafts. Mainly we just used the poles to keep the rafts in the main current, and let the river control their speed. After several days of travel, Nishi ordered us to move only at night. During the daytime we hid the rafts under the brush on the riverbank and slept while scouts went out ahead.

While floating downriver, I had time to think about the kinds of problems I might run into at the trading post we were heading for. I knew it was against the law to sell guns to Indians, so I had to be careful of what I said. I also knew that it was unlikely that the Indians would take me to a place where I could escape. Actually, at that time escape did not seem important. I felt interested in what I was doing, learning jungle medicine and making caucho. Probably through the dreaming together Chief Shumu had control over how I felt about all this. He had shut off my memory of my former life.

One morning after floating all night, we pulled the flotilla up on to the riverbank and separated the caucho blocks which were then laid out in the sun to dry. The rafts were broken up and the logs scattered. I noticed that the Indians were edgy, and I thought maybe we were coming to the end of our journey. We camped for the night while the men reassembled their packs. At dawn the following morning we took off through the forest. Late that evening we came to the riverbank again and the men started threading the blocks of rubber on a long vine.

Off in the distance I thought that I heard a dog bark. In the light of a descending moon and the first streaks of dawn, the men drew around for a conference. I distinctly heard a cock crow down the river. From this I knew what the gathering on the riverbank now was all about.

Nishi, the spokesman, said to me, "We have tied all the blocks together and put them in the river. There is also a small three-log

raft, big enough for one man. If you go down along the riverbank to avoid the deep water, you will come to a Brazilian trading post around the next point of land in the river. It is a small place, two or three houses, only a few people. We will have the village surrounded. Take the caucho down and trade it for guns. Be back here not later than sunset, sooner if possible. In case of serious trouble signal us with the whistle of the eagle that we have taught you, and we will come. We outnumber those in the village three to one and the men there are few. We have studied this place well and will have it under our control while you are there." I put on the pants and shirt from my pack. They felt strange on my body. Nishi handed me a long rafting pole, and the men held the log raft as I climbed aboard. With the pole I gently pushed the raft into the shallow water, and the string of blocks on the vine rope followed.

Now came the time for me to really think about what I would find at the trading post and what I should say. I tried to remember the few words of Portuguese I had learned with my Peruvian companions on our way up the Jurua River at least two years earlier. I had lost track of time except as the Indians marked its passage. It seemed to me best to say as little as possible in spite of my desire to ask questions to learn what was going on in the world outside my forest home.

As I came around the point of land sticking out into the river, the sun was just coming up over the forest. There in the cove I saw the small village on the riverbank just as Nishi had told me, a clearing with a group of several palm-thatched houses. Smoke rose out of the roofs of two of them. On the riverbank I saw a man drawing a bucket of water. When this man looked up and saw someone coming, he rushed up to one of the houses with his bucket of water.

By the time the man came back I had started tying up my raft at the canoe landing.

"*Bom dia,*" (good day), he called out to me.

"*Bom dia,*" I responded.

"Caucho for sale?" the man asked.
"Yes."
"Where from?"
"Upriver."
"You can trade it here—no need to go farther down."
"Good. You have rifles?"

"Just got a shipment in."

"Winchester?"

"Yes, of course."

I began to pull up the string of rubber blocks to tie it securely.

"Well-made blocks," the man said, "must be nearly a ton. I will send a man down to help you bring them up to the scales."

It took the two of us until mid-morning to carry the blocks up to the deposit shed where the scales stood. Then, with the trader, we started weighing each block. Before we started I tested the beam scales for balance, and the trader noticed.

"What price?" I asked. From the reply it seemed to me that the price had gone up since I had entered the forest on the Jurua River.

It took until midday to weigh all the blocks. During this time I had to fend off a thousand questions with one-word replies—where was my caucho camp, how many people, all Peruvians? I was anxious to get it over with and make my purchases. We went into the store to check the tally—well over a thousand pounds.

First I bought a box of rifles and checked each of the six in the box to be sure of the quality, then ten axes, twenty machetes, new pants and shirt, mirrors, knives, and beads.

After the purchases, a middle-aged Brazilian woman brought in lunch. I thought then of my mother, wondering how she was and if she thought me dead. For a moment I missed her terribly and wished I could go home to her. But that was impossible.

The trader and I ate Brazilian black bean stew, *feijoada completa,* a complete meal with rice, beans, and meat of several kinds. It tasted good, different from Indian food, and reminded me of my past.

As we ate I had to fend off many more questions.

"When will you be back with more caucho?"

"Soon."

"Seen any Indians?"

"A few."

"Any trouble with them?"

"No."

"Well, be careful, they are dangerous around here."

"So...."

From a calendar on the wall I could tell that it was June and that I had been away from home about two and a half years. There were a thousand questions I wanted to ask, but did not because of the complications that might develop from my asking. It did come out in my conversation with the trader that I was dealing with Antonio Rodrigues, of Luzero-Rodrigues da Costa Company of Manaus, Brazil, and the trading post was located on the Purus River near the border between Peru and Brazil.

It took until the middle of the afternoon to tally up the rubber and my purchases. When it was done I asked, "You interested in more caucho from my camp?"

"Of course, any time."

The balance of money after paying for the purchases came to a considerable amount, and I was not sure how to handle it. Money where I was going had no value, but I thought that maybe I could leave it on deposit at the trading post.

Finally Rodrigues himself suggested it. "Look, if you are coming back, I can open up a book for you and hold your balance for purchases in the future. Just give me your name to put in the account book." We agreed and I signed the book with a halting, unpracticed hand beside the balance.

"Can your man take me around the point upriver with my purchases in your canoe?" I asked.

"But of course, if that's what you want."

Another hour to load the canoe and shove off. When I finally arrived back where I had started out in the morning it was near sundown. Not a sign nor whisper of sound or other evidence of my companions, but a familiar birdcall from the forest indicated the Indians were nearby.

The two of us unloaded the canoe on the riverbank, and the man from the trading post returned downriver. As soon as the canoe disappeared around the point of land the Indians swarmed out of the forest. We made a rush to get the purchases out of sight and get going before we could be discovered or followed. The loads were small and light compared to the packs of rubber we had brought. As our group melted into the forest I felt the tension go out of my body. I took off my clothing and again became a part of the forest.

As we moved through the undergrowth, I began to feel distress in my stomach. When we stopped for the night I had cramps and diarrhea. For over two years I had eaten only the natural things from the forest and nothing seasoned with salt. The rich stew at the trading post had caused my upset stomach. The Indians immediately suspected poison, but I assured them that I had not been poisoned. In the morning Nishi prepared an herbal concoction for me to drink, and the trouble went away.

We stayed away from the river going back. It took us ten days at a forced pace, but we did not travel at night. On the return trip I made an effort to observe all of the natural features of the forest and land, sure that I would be traveling the route again. From the talk of my companions I was also sure that the route and the trading post had been well scouted out in advance of our trip.

The pace picked up on the last day of the trek back and one of the party went ahead to advise the chief of our pending arrival. As our group entered the village clearing a shout went up from the assembled tribe, and the packers replied with another. The chief came directly to me for his greeting, and the whole tribe gathered around. Chief Shumu ordered the pack loads put in front of him. With a large circle of onlookers watching, he and I unpacked the new guns first. A gasp of admiration went up from the crowd at the sight of them.

The chief made a speech. "These will defend us from our enemies," he said. "You have seen what happens when they speak with

the voice of thunder. We will dominate the forest and live without fear. You know who got these for us." The Indians shouted as Chief Shumu put his hand on my shoulder.

"We can get more of them when needed. Other things can come to us from the caucho. Let me show you." Then the chief opened the other loads. They unwrapped the axes and the machetes, and he told the crowd: "With these we will produce more caucho to buy more guns, and these tools will make it easier to clear the ground for our gardens."

The packages of knickknacks also created a sensation among the people—the beads, fish hooks, and mirrors. The women were especially delighted with the varicolored beads. But the real sensation came when both the men and women realized that they could see themselves in the several small mirrors that I had brought to them.

Everything was community property, and all of it was passed around for everyone to see. When all had looked to their satisfaction, everything came back to Chief Shumu for his final disposal of the items among the various houses of the village.

Our return with new treasures was good reason for a celebration. Preparation for body painting got underway. Use of the mirrors to inspect and modify the face and body decorations soon became an exciting diversion. The women were the experts at painting, but they got lots of advice from the men. They took a great deal of care using both black and red paint to produce original designs. The results often gave a striking effect with dots, wavy and zigzag lines, and various geometric forms. Each artist had a distinctive style. The women took great pride in this work and were complimented by the men for their efforts.

In addition, the women wore wide necklaces and arm bands of beads and animal teeth and the men wore headbands of flaring, brightly colored feathers that gave the effect of wearing a brilliant crown. These were all made by the women. Also the men often placed bright feathers in their perforated earlobes, noses, and lower lips. Some of them had feathered arm and leg bands. When the tribe assembled, fully decorated for a celebration, they filled the village with a gay, strikingly colorful menagerie.

While we had been gone, the women had prepared large jars of fermented beverages and cut large piles of firewood. At sundown the men kindled several small fires to light the dancing area between the houses. Chief Shumu appeared from his house dressed in his ceremonial shirt decorated now with brilliant feathers woven into the cotton fabric. In one hand he held a dance leader's baton—a short stick with a string having a tuft of feathers attached to the end. At a sign from the chief the women passed around cups of the fermented drink. The men tied strings of rattles around their ankles, and soon the chants started.

The actual dancing began little by little after the chanting had gone on for some time. At a signal from Chief Shumu the men and women formed a line, alternating men and women, and joined arms at the elbows. At the beginning the chief led the line in a slow chanting snake dance. As the dancing became livelier he handed the baton to a younger man to lead. The tribe had many different chants and dances. The dances changed in tempo and mood with the changes in the chants.

Every two or three hours the dancers would pause to cool off. Then the fermented drinks would be passed around again. By morning some showed the effects of drunkenness, but the drinking and dancing went on. After two days and nights of drinking and dancing, the celebration stopped and everyone rested for a day. Then they all went back to work at their usual duties of gathering food from the forest, gardening, and hunting.

The new axes and machetes from the trading post made the preparation and tending of the family garden plots much easier than when they had only stone tools. The men did the work of cutting the forest and clearing new garden plots for the women to plant. The tree and brush cutting took place during the dry season, and everything was left to dry in the sun. They burned it all, and planting took place at the end of the dry season, just before the rains started. The women did the important work of planting, tending, and harvesting the garden produce. Chief Shumu predicted the weather so that they could do these tasks at just the right time.

The village was located along the crest of a series of hills, and this made the horizon across the forest visible in clear weather. The chief used the progress of the sun and moon in relation to points on the horizon to judge the approximate beginning and ending of each dry season. He also observed the behavior of the vegetation and animals for clues to more specific timing of climatic events of each season.

One dark night during a long tedious rainy spell that made outside work difficult, the chief predicted the beginning of the dry season within days. This made everyone happy, but the joy was short-lived. The call of a night bird brought an immediate wave of fear and dismay among the people. Around first one house and then another in the village sounded the ominous call of *"Chieu, chieu, chieu."* This, I found out, was the call of a small unseen night bird of ill omen. If it persisted, the call was a sure sign of death in the village. The only remedy came from building many fires outside and burning hot peppers on the fires. The stinging fumes might drive the unwelcome visitor away.

Now the people scrambled to build fires near each house. Soon eye-burning fumes billowed up around the village. The bird, however, stayed. He seemed to avoid the stinging smoke, and his piercing call echoed through the village again and again. Gloom settled over the people and remained even after the offending cry finally faded into the night.

A few days later, the *"chieu, chieu"* visit forgotten, a group of men were building hunting blinds in a tall fruit tree in the forest. The beginning of the dry season brought on a time of intense hunting activity, because many trees produced ripe fruit at this time, attracting birds and animals.

Somehow a young man working on a shooting blind in the treetop slipped and fell a hundred feet to the ground. He died before his companions could reach his side. When word came back, the entire village reacted.

A group of men brought the body back and placed it in a sitting position on a small bench against a tree. The women prepared a liquid extract from huito leaves and fruit. With this the men and women of the whole village painted their bodies black, making strange designs on their faces. The family, chanting a sad dirge and wailing, led the rest of the tribe to the sitting figure. There, wailing and weeping, they knelt and touched their foreheads to the ground before the silent figure.

Then an old woman brought a large burial urn. Inside this they placed the body, knees drawn up under the chin, and put in all of the young hunter's personal possessions. Placing another jar over the mouth of the urn, they then buried it deep in the ground near the village, with great lamentation and mournful chanting.

This death was not an event quickly forgotten, especially within the young man's family. Each time they had occasion to recall the dead man, his mother and brothers would go to the grave, sighing and making personal requests of the dead one almost as if they considered him off on a trip, soon to return.

Others would also come, and all together they would return to the village, talking about the departed one and remembering events of his life.

The family started food plants around the grave, and tended them with care in case he needed food. Only little by little did they forget their sadness, as daily happenings in the village obscured the memory.

12

Myths and Legends

On Where the Huni Kui Came From

SOMETIMES, WHEN CONDITIONS were just right in the village, Chief Shumu could be led by careful prompting into telling stories. One evening a large group assembled on the hill between the houses. Seated in comfort on woven mats and animal skins, they admired the clear dry-season night sky. The discussion centered on the stars and the probable time for the beginning of the coming rainy season. The talk drifted to felling and burning the forest for new garden plots. This led the old chief to telling tribal history. The story was an old one the villagers knew well. A sigh of pleasure passed through the listeners as he began:

"In the dim and ancient past beyond recall, when man could still talk with the animals, our people had many houses and lived in peace with an abundance of everything they needed. They lacked nothing and lived in happiness on the sandy shore where the great water reached out until it touched the sky.

"One day there came a great storm, worse than anyone had ever seen before. Everything stopped and all the people went to their houses. Thunder and lightning came with a terrible wind that destroyed all the houses.

"The sky broke and fell down. The earth crumbled and went up into the sky. Everything died except some crabs in a hole. Then the sky returned to its place and took the spirits of the dead with it into the new sky. There they lived happily, but on the earth nothing remained but a few crabs.

"Then after a long time, one day the lightning opened up a crack in the sky, and a woman fell out onto the land. She was killed by the fall. A crab living in a hole nearby came out and found the woman. With the knife in his claw he opened up her belly and found twins, a boy and a girl.

"The crab raised them, and he called the boy Shaka (Crab), the girl Mashi (Good). They had a family which grew and grew and became the Huni Kui. Some animals came down from the sky again, too. But people found that they could no longer talk with them.

"People then did not die as we do now. Their spirits just turned into new bodies. Old men changed to boys, old women into girls. On the earth no darkness existed. Troublemakers like the wasp, stinging ants, mosquitoes, and biting flies were found only on a small island in the center of the great water.

"Shaka had many sons, one named Poka. He in turn had a son, Mana, along with others. Now Mana found life too boring, always the same. For fun he went to the boa who gave him a butterfly. A small alligator went out to the island in the great water and brought back to Mana a wasp, a mosquito, and a fly. The spider gave him a small flask with darkness inside. Mana opened up the flask and darkness came out. That's when night began.

"It took the people a long time to understand the darkness. They were afraid of it. Someone complained to Poka, Mana's father. Then Poka called Mana and asked him why he had caused this terrible thing—the darkness.

"Mana became troubled, then angry. 'I will show the people how to understand it,' he shouted.

"Poka at that time was a very old man, and because of the trouble over the darkness, Mana angrily asked his father when he would die.

"The old man said, 'Bring me poison and I will die now.'

"Mana went to the forest and found a small poisonous toad which he took to his father. Poka swallowed the toad without washing it. Then he became so sick he could not stand up. At sunset he called his son and said, 'You have killed me. I am going to die and go up into the sky. As I go I will call back and give instructions about how you must continue to live on the earth.'

"That night the old man died. In the morning it began to thunder, and the wind came up as Poka went up into the sky. He kept calling back, 'Change—change your skin,' until he was gone and they could hear him no longer. With all the thunder and wind the people heard him wrong and thought he said, 'Stay—stay where you are.'

"They heard it wrong. It was a terrible mistake. The snakes understood well, also the spider, the wood tick, the locust, and the *pau mulato* tree. These all change their skins and never die.

"Before all this, when Poka deliberately took poison, our people did not die. They lived in happiness with no trouble or pain until the argument over the darkness. When the old man died from poison, the people heard him wrong. If they had heard right, as did some of the animals, we would not have to die now. We could change our skins like the snakes do. But now it is too late. Our bodies get tired with old skin and we die. If we could change our skin, pain would not bother us, and we could go on living as we like. It was a terrible mistake when they heard wrong, a mistake that sealed the fate of us all.

"Of our own people, the Huni Kui, the first was Harucun, called Tiwa by his people. He was born not far from the great water that touches the sky. There on the bank of the rough sea he was born and lived.

"After him, Apo, the Angry One the people called Shano, was born. They lived together.

"Tiwa, the first, married a beautiful woman and lived with her there beside the water. Shano, the Angry One, lived with Tiwa, but without a woman. Later Shano moved away. Tiwa with his wife raised our people. From Shano, the Angry One, came other people

"When he was growing up Tiwa liked the *jacy* palm nuts. Shano preferred the seed of the *shabo,* the *uricury* palm. Tiwa liked his people. He kept them together in a village. They made large clearings and planted crops that they enjoyed as they lived together. They lived and ate well in their good village. They worked hard building their houses on the sandy shore of the great water that reached out to touch the sky. In happiness they lived and stayed well.

"Shano, the Angry One, without a wife, lived with his people not far away in the same way.

"Tiwa's wife was a very beautiful woman, and one day Shano came and made love to her. When Tiwa found out, he became very angry and told Shano he would punish him for what he had done to his wife. Then Shano, mean and angry, left and armed himself with his lance, bow and arrows, and his club.

"When Shano returned to Tiwa's house, Tiwa was seated alone with his wife eating. The Angry One, Shano, said, 'Tiwa, your woman is very beautiful and I like her. Why do you threaten to kill me?'

"Tiwa replied, 'You live with your people without a wife. Among your people there are many, many women. They abound in your village. You take none of your women for a wife. Why? To be free? Why do you come to make love to my woman? For adventure? Among your people women are abundant, but you are not married. So you want my woman for adventure. You came and took my woman, so I will come and take all the women of your people.'

"Shano, the Angry One, went into a rage. He shouted, 'For what you say I will kill you!'

"Tiwa jumped up and ran for his bow and arrows, but Shano had come already armed. He shot two arrows and hit Tiwa in the heart.

Tiwa did not have time to shoot but shouted as he fell.

"Tiwa's people were all at work in their gardens. Tiwa's wife became afraid. She shouted and shouted. The people heard and came, wondering what had happened.

"Then Shano became frightened and ran away.

"As the people began to come they found Tiwa in his house, stretched out on the floor dead. His wife stood there alone, crying. They asked her, 'Who killed him, our chief, and ran away? What happened?'

"She told them how it had all happened, and Tiwa's people wept. The children, the women, and the men all shed tears.

"Then the men got together and said, 'Let us go and do the same to Shano. He came here without provocation and killed our great chief. In return we must go do the same to Shano, the mean and angry one.'

"All together with their arms they went. The women stayed guarding the village. Shano knew, of course, that they would come. He armed his people and waited.

"Tiwa's people were very many, Shano's not so many. Tiwa's men were strong, not afraid; they went well armed, shouting and shouting, and shooting arrows. They fought and fought, Tiwa's men against those of Shano. Some on both sides were wounded, some died, some were not hurt. After a long battle both sides withdrew. Tiwa's men went home to have a battle dance; Shano's people did the same.

"Tiwa was dead. His people battled for his honor with grief in their hearts. Now they laid out the body in his house. The king vulture came as a messenger from the sky. With a basket on his back he took the soul of Harucun, called Tiwa the first, ancestor of the Huni Kui, to the dwelling place of spirits in the sky. Thunder rumbled the entire day. As the soul of Tiwa rose into the sky the thunder rumbled time after time.

"The people buried the body, and it turned into earth. Tiwa's peo-

ple came together and decided to leave the place of their bad luck. They migrated up the rivers. In grief they fought, and then migrated away from the place of their misfortune.

"If Shano had not killed Tiwa without reason there where our people were born, we would still be living happily in the fine village, by the great rough water that reaches out to touch the sky. But Tiwa was killed; his people fought with grief and courage and were scattered up many rivers. Thus our own people, the Huni Kui, came to the river Honowa-ia, the Tarauaca.

"Shano's people left also and went up other rivers.

"Our people now living on many different rivers all speak the same language.

"From the other rivers, Shano's people now speak another language.

"That is the story of how our great chief Tiwa was killed." Then Chief Shumu added, "At our villages on the River Honowa-ia where we lived, our people were attacked by the rubber cutters. Many were killed and the children carried away. We had to leave again and hide in the forest. The Ishabo and Shabo people came here earlier into the depths of the forest. We found them and they let us join with them. Now we are one, the Donowan (Boa People). Long ago when our people first came to Honowa-ia under their new chief Ino, they learned how to dream together to find out how to live in a new place. Remember that with the few who did not die after the rubber cutters attacked our villages, we used dreaming together to find the Ishabo and Shabo here where we now live, the Place to Begin Again that we call Shanada.

With the storytelling finished, the people drifted a few at a time back to their houses and left Chief Shumu looking at the night sky for signs of when the rains would begin.

13

Marriage and Family

On My Attachment to the Huni Kui

THE DAY NATAKOA, one of the best hunters of the village, and his wife Yawanini came to the chief to discuss the selection of a girl for their eldest son, it became an event of interest to all the village. A marriage provided the occasion for the tribe's favorite dance celebration A young man's family usually took the first step toward arranging a marriage. Chief Shumu had heard from one of his old women about the problem of selecting a girl, and he expected Natakoa with his wife. The meeting was arranged for a proper and unhurried discussion.

Natakoa began by saying, "You may remember when my first-born, a strong boy, was given his first bath and you brushed him with the fragrant leaves that keep away the evil spirits. He did not cry out as most newborns do but waved his arms and legs with great vigor. Besides his secret name which no one utters, we call him Nawatoto (Hawk). He learned to walk sooner than most. When I gave him his first small bow and blunt arrow, the pet animals around the village soon found it wise to stay out of his range

"As soon as he was big enough to hunt in the edge of the forest with the other small boys, he usually led the group and never came back without something valuable from the forest. When he had

strength enough to go with me into the forest, I found that he learned quickly and remembered from one hunt to the next whatever I had taught him.

"Now he has reached the age and has the experience to go into the forest alone. With his hunting and mine, our family has more food than we need. I notice that he sometimes becomes restless. At night he often talks in his sleep. These are signs that now he needs a wife to start a family of his own."

Chief Shumu glanced at Yawanini and she said, "He has been a vigorous, busy boy, and we hope that you can give him a girl who will raise a good family for him. We think he is ready."

The chief then spoke to Natakoa. "Send the boy to your hunting territory tomorrow. In the afternoon bring him here to show me the game he found and the weapons he used. We will see if he is ready to support a woman by himself. After that we can discuss it further, and then I will see which one of the girls his age might make him a good wife if he is ready."

The next afternoon the boy called Hawk came with his parents to the chief's house. With him he brought the game he had killed during the morning hunt, a large *coata* monkey and a partridge. He also carried his lance, bow and arrows, and bamboo knife.

First Chief Shumu looked over the weapons and commented on several defects he found. Then he examined the animals. The partridge's legs were broken, and the young man's face was marked with blood, now dried and flaking off. The chief questioned the boy for a long time about the habit of each animal he brought and also about other animals of the forest.

No decision came from this first discussion. That would come at a later meeting between the chief and Nawatoto's father, Natakoa. But everyone present felt satisfied that the young hunter had done well. A few days later Natakoa and Chief Shumu met again, and the chief told Natakoa about the girl he thought would be a good wife for Nawatoto. Natakoa came from the palm-tree people, the Shabo, and Shumu suggested a girl named Irikina, a member of the Donowan group, whose people had come from the Tarauaca River. Before making a final decision, the chief consulted with a group of older men and women of the tribe, as well as with the families on both sides of the match.

Finally, after all the discussions, and when everyone had agreed that this would make a good marriage, Chief Shumu gave his final decision and set forth all the conditions which must be met before the marriage could take place. These preparations would take several weeks, and Chief Shumu kept a careful watch over everything done for the big event.

The hunters prepared a large store of smoked game for the days of the marriage celebration, when no hunting would be done. The old women started the preparation of large jars of strong brew, adding sugarcane juice to the mixture of fruit juices. They buried the jars in the ground with only the necks sticking out and left the mixture to ferment for several days. When ready, this strong liquor produced a slow but intense drunkenness if consumed in large quantities.

Ten days before the time set for the marriage ceremony, the women prepared an extract from the leaves and fruit of the huito tree. The men and women both had their bodies painted with this extract, and in a couple of days the skin of our bodies turned black. A few days later this black skin peeled off, leaving new skin free of blemishes. This made a good base for decorative body paint. The painting of fantastic designs on our bodies began a couple of days before the marriage. The women specialized in the art of body painting, using huito extract for black lines and achiote for the red figures. The results were spectacular. The women also made striking feathered headbands for the young couple, along with arm and leg bands of bright feathers. During the final days of body painting and the making of strands of beads and feather decorations by the women, excitement grew more

and more intense as the Huni Kui got ready for their favorite celebration. When the body paint and the feathered decorations were all
in order to the satisfaction of the women, the chief ordered the men
to bring together the large baskets of smoked meat they had been
preparing for several days.

The ceremony started late in the afternoon of the appointed day.
At a signal from the chief, Nawatoto's and Irikina's families brought
the young pair before the assembled crowd. Chief Shumu, dressed
in a brilliant feathered robe and headdress, held a ceremonial bow
and arrow in one hand. He motioned for the young couple to stand
before him with joined hands. Then he gave a short lecture on how
they should conduct their lives. At the end of this, Irikina brought
the chief a bowl full of fermented drink from the first jug of liquor,
and a shout went up from the villagers. The second cup she took to
her new husband. Then drinks were passed around to everyone, and
the celebration got underway.

Chanting started right away and dancing soon followed. Chief
Shumu chanted and joined in the dancing, actively engaging in the
celebration until the young couple had drunk several bowls of the
liquor and began to show the effects. Then he went to his nearby
hammock and watched over the party. About this time several of the
older women of the tribe loudly offered their drunken and ribald
advice on how the newlyweds should conduct their affairs. A roar of
laughter went up when Nawakano, the bride's mother, offered her
advice. Festivities continued day and night as long as the food and
liquor lasted—several days. Toward the end, arguments among the
men started, but Chief Shumu always settled these before any violence broke out.

The village organized this same kind of a celebration when Chief
Shumu gave Huaini (Fragrant Flower) to me shortly after I returned
from trading caucho for guns. Huaini was the girl who attended me
when I was first brought to the village after my capture in the cau-

cho camp. She had smiled at me when I drank the sweet banana drink she brought me after I refused the sour, fermented yucca drink she had first brought. After that, Huaini had been the one to bring my food to me during those first few days in the strange village. With her shy smiles and other attentions, she helped me through that time of deep depression and fear.

Shumu had watched with satisfaction as an obviously strong feeling of affection grew between us. With everyone happy about the trade goods that I had brought from the trading post, the time was right for chief to arrange for our marriage ceremony and celebration. I had reached the age of about seventeen at the time. To me, Chief Shumu's satisfaction about joining us together was obvious. After all, by this time he and I had been with each other in dreaming together on many occasions. I had shared his thoughts as he had shared mine. Now I could tell that he felt for sure that I would stay and take his place as leader of his people. That I had now taken one of them as my most intimate companion was no idle gesture.

Chief Shumu must have acknowledged in his own mind the risks of taking in a stranger from a different culture to train as a leader for his people. He no doubt weighed that risk against the possibility of his people losing their leadership without the help that I could bring. If that happened, they would lose the main base for their understanding of the lore of the jungle. This made it possible for them to live in harmony with the complexity, beyond common understanding, of how the tropical forest worked. The chief must have also understood the risk that I undertook following the lure of adventure, along with the attraction of the mystery and magic of the black jaguar. All of which brought me into the realm of his influence. It also seemed to me that he may have had some influence over these events. Now it remained for both of us to see how this would all play out in the daily course of our lives.

By the usual village custom, a young married couple went to live in the house of the mother of the bride, where all their needs were taken care of until the first child was born. After that the young couple entered the tribal life, and the young man cleared a garden plot in the forest for his wife and hunted for the game they needed. Because of my special position in the tribe, when Huaini and I were married we stayed in the chief's house, and I went on with my training with the chief. By now it was obvious to everyone in the village that Chief Shumu expected me to follow in his role as tribal shaman or medicine man. With this role of leadership came the implied obligation to pass the knowledge along to an apprentice. In this way the lore would not be lost.

14

Jaguars

On Dominating a Fearful Beast

THE BIRTH OF A child took place in the forest. The mother usually gave birth alone or was assisted by another woman if needed. If the firstborn of a family was a boy, special ceremonies were held, including several herbal baths made from leaves and tree barks. Each bath had its special chant, sung as the materials were gathered and the extracts prepared, as well as while the child was being bathed. The chants were thought to increase the effectiveness of the treatment and were designed to give the new boy fearlessness, good hunting ability, physical strength, and stamina.

To mark the special occasion of our firstborn boy, Chief Shumu ordered him to be baptized with the blood of the jaguar. The jaguar was the largest and most dangerous animal in the forest. These Indians had many stories and legends of disastrous encounters with the beast. They also greatly admired its hunting powers and its ability to dominate all the other animals of the forest. This admiration accounted for the ceremonial use of jaguar blood on special occasions, such as the baptism of a boy expected to take an important place in the future of the tribe.

To prepare, the chief called the best hunters together to determine

where the most recent signs of the spotted jaguar had been seen and to decide on the best location for the hunt. Chief Shumu included me in the group of six hunters who left one morning before dawn, well armed with bows and arrows. A silent mist drifted through the forest as we departed. Every leaf hung ready to scatter cold drops of dew on us as we passed. By this time I felt at home in the forest. We had spent the night chanting and taking special herbal baths to eliminate all body odors that might alert our prey.

We traveled in single file, going south to a familiar hunting area of long low hills and valleys. Just before sunrise we stopped and carefully chose our hunting ground. We needed a group of medium-sized trees with branches barely above the reach of the jaguar and a large tree nearby with its crown well above the rest of the forest. The ground vegetation had to be open enough so that we could see the jaguar when it arrived within range.

We chose our vantage points in the low branches with care and cut some leafy branches to help cover up our presence. When the others were ready, the jaguar caller went up a vine to the top of the tall tree that stood out over the rest of the forest. He took a small clay jug into which he would blow to imitate jaguar sounds. The hunters on the lower branches arranged bird calls to signal the jaguar caller of the critical stages of the hunt, such as no sign yet of the jaguar, signs of his coming, the direction of his approach, and jaguar in sight. By this time the sky showed streaks of sunlight and the forest began to come alive with daytime sounds of birds and animals.

The jaguar caller had to get above the forest canopy for his calls to reach any distance. The thick leafy vegetation of the forest floor absorbs sounds near the ground and they do not carry far. Soon the wavering, wailing call of the cat floated out over the forest from the treetop caller and his jug. A bird trill of approval came from one of the Indians, but there was no other sound for some minutes. The jaguar call had to be repeated several times. As time passed, the tension built up among the bowmen in the tree branches.

The first signal of the approach of a jaguar came from a group of the smallest jungle partridges. These small birds never fly up except when a jaguar approaches them. Otherwise they prefer to run on the ground. Now, from out of sight, the hunters all heard the sound of the explosive take-off of the birds. Bird calls passed among the tree branches to indicate the direction from which the cat approached. In the treetop the jaguar caller changed his tone to soft grunts. These soon brought an answer from a short distance away, from an animal still out of sight. Then we all heard the repeated call, *"Chee, chee,"* from a little bird that nearly always follows any jaguar.

Suddenly, seemingly from nowhere, a tremendous spotted animal stood in an open place just below the watchers, looking up into the trees, growling. Almost in unison the bowstrings twanged from several directions. As soon as the arrows struck, we slithered down from our perches.

When hit, the jaguar sprang straight up in the air and fell back writhing on the ground. Immediately one Indian put a vine loop around his hind feet and stretched them backward to a tree trunk tie. Another did the same with the front feet, and a hitch was put around the head to stretch out the neck. By this time the caller had come slithering down a vine from his treetop, his calling jug in one hand. We soon had the jug full of jaguar blood from a cut in the animal's neck. Placing a stopper in the jug, the party broke up. Two of us rushed back to the village to deliver the jaguar blood before it could dry up. The others remained behind to remove the prized teeth and claws.

The villagers waited anxiously, and gave a shout when we two arrived. At once the jaguar chant began, and the chief anointed my newborn son with the blood of the valiant jaguar. Huaini proudly stood by with a smile on her face. Chief Shumu gave the boy the name of Iria (Leader), and predicted he would be a good hunter and

show leadership ability in the future. Then he handed the infant back to his mother.

Jaguars were not abundant in the forest, but an occasional encounter kept the hunters alert to recognizing the signs and being prepared. The accumulated knowledge of the tribe about this animal was circulated in the stories told around the fire at night to educate the young men. The important tactic of an actual encounter with a jaguar was to keep the animal off balance and unready to attack. This could be done by throwing things, making unexpected sounds, dropping a piece of game, and dodging out of sight. In combat on the ground the lance was the best weapon. If one could get up a tree out of reach, then a bow and arrow could be used, but it was extremely dangerous to be on the ground with an arrow-wounded jaguar.

One evening at dusk in our village, a faint wailing sounded off in the distance. The chief sent several men out to investigate. Soon one of them rushed back to say that one of the hunters was dragging himself home with his body badly ripped apart.

Chief Shumu gave a flurry of orders, and the people rushed to carry them out. Various types of green herbs were gathered, and preparations of medicine had already begun when the men arrived carrying the half-dead hunter, obviously mangled by a jaguar. His scalp hung half loose and his back and shoulders were covered with terrible bleeding rips and gashes.

The man seemed barely conscious, but drank a portion of water and ground herbs the chief held to his lips. Then we laid him out on a floor mat in the chief's house. There, the long process of repair and recovery began. Chief Shumu, after carefully examining the wounds, ordered one of his old women to polish black palm thorns. While this was being done, he applied a poultice of crushed herbs to the wounds. The process took several hours, during which the victim showed but few signs of life as his wounds were pinned shut with the thorns.

I sat up with the chief all night chanting and watching the patient for favorable signs. In the morning the chief sent a party of the best trackers to backtrack the wounded hunter's trail and, if possible, learn what had happened. The hunter himself remained unconscious.

At midday the trackers came back with the body of a deer and the teeth and claws of a jaguar. The bloody trail over which the mauled hunter had dragged himself had not been difficult to follow. The men had found the deer hanging in a small tree. In the bushes nearby they found the body of a jaguar killed by a deep knife gash in his shoulder that had penetrated to the heart. Going farther in the forest, the men found signs that the jaguar had been following the hunter since he had killed the deer.

The hunter's painful recovery took a long time. As he slowly came back to life, the Indians gave him a new name—Ino Doto, Jaguar Killer. When he could talk, the story gradually came out.

"I killed the deer about sunset and started back home. On the way a large band of monkeys went by high overhead in the treetops. My attempt to stop them and call them down did not work, and I could not follow them with the deer hanging on my shoulder. So I threw a vine over a limb and pulled the deer up into a small tree. Then I tried to follow the monkeys, but they soon scattered and were lost in the treetops before I could get off an arrow.

"Darkness deepened as I returned, disappointed, to my deer. When I came to the tree where I had pulled it up for protection, there was a movement. Too close and too late to draw an arrow to my bow, I realized that a jaguar stood there on his hind feet reaching for my deer. He turned with a loud snarling growl and came spitting at me, standing on his two back feet. As he put one paw on my shoulder and the claws dug in, I just barely managed to maneuver a small tree between us. He could not bite me, but his breath in my face had a hideous stink. As he reached for me with his other set of claws, I managed to free the bamboo knife from the string around my neck,

and struck his shoulder as he ripped my head and shoulders with his claws. Once or twice my knife went deep and I turned it before striking again.

"With a terrible scream he broke free, taking my knife with him, and went thrashing and wailing into the bushes. Blood from my head wounds blinded my eyes, but I knew that if I was to survive I had to get back quickly to the chief for his medicine. The trip back became worse than a nightmare of pain and confusion. As my strength gave out from the loss of blood I began shouting, hoping to get help before I fell and died on the trail. If you had not heard me calling, I would have died there. But I knew that if I could get back to the chief, he would not let me die."

After a long period of recovery, the jaguar slayer remained a semi-invalid. Because of the damage to his shoulder and arm muscles he was never able to pull a bowstring or hunt again. He made himself useful around the village, and his sons helped provide game, while his wife and daughters worked to produce other needed food in their gardens and from the forest.

The women of the tribe carried out many important functions that kept the community working efficiently. They planted and cared for the gardens, harvesting the crops and gathering food from the forest. The fresh game brought in by the men from the forest was turned over to the women, either to be prepared for preservation by smoking or cooked for food. The women also prepared all the food from the garden produce and saw to it that the men had food when they came in from a long hunt or other strenuous work like clearing a new garden plot. Weaving hammocks and cloth and pottery-making were also important tasks performed by the women.

15

Assassin

Rivalry for Jungle Territory

THE HUNI KUI, as they called themselves, were true forest dwellers, as you can see from my story so far. The villages led by Chief Shumu, and which I came to know, were set in a series of small forest clearings surrounded by a vast expanse of unbroken forest. Their primitive agriculture was adapted to small jungle clearings that they moved to new locations as the soil became exhausted after two or three years of cultivation.

Hunting and food-gathering activities actually resulted in the villages spending more time in the forest than in their villages. The forest in its undisturbed state was made up of several distinct though partly mixed layers of vegetation. A few scattered forest giants towered over the rest of the jungle, and under the shadow of these great trees was a thick, dense layer of medium to large trees. Below this there grew a layer of small trees and shrubs, and finally the low ground plants. The Indians gathered food from every part of this varied world—animals, birds, eggs, reptiles, insects, honey, leaves, flowers and fruit, tubers and roots.

With my intensive training I soon felt as much at home in the forest as my captors. I could go off with a small group of companions to hunt, gather fruit, and spend the whole day or several days and nights in the forest. I could cover great distances and find my way back to the village or wherever I wanted to go, without assistance. Chief Shumu observed all this. I knew that the old man said to himself with satisfaction, "He is as one of us now. With Huaini he will stay with us always and make a good chief for my people."

One day I was off several hours from the village with Huaini and two of the young girl companions the chief had given me. We had separated from a small group who were cutting caucho for the next trip to the trading post. It was time for a certain well-known fruit tree, the caimito, to be in full fruit, and we expected to gather some for the village. We had found the tree and I had climbed up into the branches when a tremendous arrow struck and lodged in a tree limb just beside my shoulder, barely missing me. I immediately swung around to the other side of the tree trunk, and, with a warning shout, slid down a vine to the ground. There I grabbed my rifle and sent a couple of shots off in the direction from which the arrow had come. We could see no one in the dense vegetation.

Hearing the shots and the commotion, the nearby rubber cutters came to see what had happened. They brought the arrow down and examined it. None of them had seen an arrow like it before. They sent out trackers to investigate, while the others rushed with me back to the village. Our arrival and the news caused an uproar.

The chief called all the men together and organized several search parties to try to determine the source of this attempt on my life. The best trackers of the village could find no track to follow. As the days passed and the search parties returned, tension and frustration grew. Nothing could be found, but something had to be done.

Now the chief called the men together for a tobacco juice talk. He told his old women to prepare a liquid extract of tobacco and other herbs. This he put in a shallow dish and the men gathered around it. Each of them in turn put his finger in the dish and then licked off the liquid. The talk among us built up slowly along with the tobacco intoxication, all guided by Chief Shumu. The chief reminded the men of their obligation to protect the tribe, especially from the attacks of the hated Shaawo, the Macaw people, who in the past had often killed our men and carried off our women. Each man, the chief told them, carried a family obligation to avenge past attacks on their relatives. He reminded each one in the group of specific deaths in their family history that had still not been properly and fully accounted for. The chief implicated in some way every man listening to him.

Then he harangued them with a tale that revealed to me for the first time the whole story of my presence among them. "I am an old man," Chief Shumu said. "Without a strong chief you will live like animals in the forest, fighting among yourselves. Remember this is not the first time that a young man whom I have carefully prepared to be your chief after I am gone has been attacked in the forest. You will recall that my only surviving son was assassinated in the forest when he became ready to be your leader. This was not so long ago and you should remember it well. My sorrow at the loss goes beyond the telling of words, and I have not forgotten."

An angry muttering went through the crowd, but Chief Shumu went on saying, "I am an old man. My flesh and bones grow tired. I cannot change my skin. Our ancestors heard wrong, and we lost the secret.

"Remember, dreaming together, we decided among ourselves to bring in a young man from outside to be our chief. I chanted to him, brought him into the forest. I told you where to find him. The right young man was to get arms for us to defend ourselves and teach us to use them on our enemies. This has now been done better than we ever expected. But if you cannot protect him, soon you will be living like a band of pigs in the forest, wandering around led by an old sow. I do not have time to train another chief for you.

"Last night I had a dream. I saw a village of the Macaw people off toward the rising sun. The attack came from there. Tomorrow I will start giving instructions for our attack. Now go prepare yourselves and your fighting equipment." The crowd of men broke up into small groups, each acting out the terrible things they would do to the enemy.

After a few days of preparation a group assembled at the chief's house and showed themselves ready for a raid on the village of my would-be assassin. They did not want me to go along because the location was so far away, and protecting me would be difficult. Chief Shumu agreed, so in my place they took two Indians whom I had trained to use the rifles.

The Indians found the rifles disappointing as weapons in the forest, because of the limited visibility. They considered the noise of the gun useful to scare an enemy, but if he dodged behind a tree he could escape. In a village clearing or garden plots, the gun proved more effective. For hunting game the gun's noise had the disadvantage of scaring other animals away.

The old chief and I waited many anxious days after the raiding party went out. Finally the chief said the party would return the next day. The women had been preparing large pots of fermented drink for the celebration of their return, but the general routine of the village had been totally upset by the expedition. Tension among those of us left behind had grown while the men were gone.

The raiding party arrived as Chief Shumu had predicted, but the raid had been a complete failure. When the party arrived at the enemy village, which they found easily from Chief Shumu's directions, it had been abandoned. Clearly the enemy had left some time earlier. The houses were falling down and rotting away. No indication remained as to where they had gone. The raiders could only turn around and come back.

This news was a very great letdown for everyone. Now we had no reason for a big victory dance. The chief did consent to a drinking bout to use up the fermented liquor the women had prepared. The drinking turned the villagers into an unruly mob. During the second day of drinking, long, involved discussions about unpleasant incidents within the tribe and between families began. Even things that had happened during the childhood of some of the older people were wrangled over as if they had happened yesterday. Accusations and lengthy arguments went on for hours as the drinking continued. Sometimes things got out of hand, and the chief would have to act to calm the people down. In the end, when the fermented drink was all gone, the arguments were settled until the next time.

Shortly after the affair of the unsuccessful raid, and perhaps because of it, a group went out on a raid without my knowing about it. Two or three weeks after the men came back, I became aware they had attacked a rubber camp because of the loot the men divided up among the villagers. By that time I knew the language well, and only had to listen carefully to know what had happened.

I went to Chief Shumu and told him that attacking rubber camps would bring bands of rubber cutters against the village in counter raids. The outsiders would have superior arms and organization and might wipe out our Indian village. Chief Shumu replied, "My people have suffered innumerable raids and atrocities at the hands of the rubber cutters before we migrated here. Men were killed, women and children carried off.

"Do you remember the old woman who wanted to kill you when you first arrived? She lost her whole family in the last raid before we moved here to the center of the forest. I knew you would never be safe in our village as long as she was alive.

"Most of the atrocities we have suffered have not been avenged in any way. The only way we can avenge ourselves for the past horrors to our people is by what these men have just done. To stop them means waiting until all the old people who have lost part of their families are gone, or at least have forgotten. You know by now that

they do not forget easily or soon." I found myself in no position to argue with the chief and said no more.

By now at least a year had passed since the first trip to the trading post to sell caucho. Production had continued off and on among the groups I had trained, and enough blocks for another trip had accumulated. The chief suggested that the tribe needed more rifles, ammunition, machetes, and other trade goods. Preparations began for the long trip to the trading post. This time I felt uneasy leaving my young family behind when I departed.

The trip turned out much the same as the previous one, except for an encounter with a party of hostile Indians. One evening as we brought the rafts of rubber blocks out of hiding under the riverbank vegetation, a warning call came from the guard on land. I was still on shore and grabbed the rifle I had brought along. Soon violent shouting and fighting broke out. I brought my rifle into play. The surprise of this caused the attackers to disappear. Three of them had been killed by the rifle shots while my group had received only light wounds.

Before the enemy could counterattack, we hastily launched the flotilla of rafts in silence. We floated through the night with everyone on board. My men told me we had been attacked by the hooded Bolanshos. They said that we had been lucky to get away with so few injuries because they were very aggressive, violent people. That night our trip was no leisurely float downriver. We used the rafting poles against the river bottom to hasten our progress and put as much distance as possible between us and our enemies. In the early dawn we tied up on the opposite side of the river and took every effort to protect ourselves. We posted guards and sent out scouts to check the riverbank downstream. Early in the afternoon, as soon as the scouts came back with an all clear signal, our rafts took off again.

At the trading post things worked out the same as on the earlier trip. I carefully revealed nothing of my connection with Indians in the forest because I knew that it would cause complications. The price of rubber had gone down. Still, the rubber I brought in earned enough credit to buy all the things we needed and to double the sum on deposit. This time I ate nothing at the post and thus avoided the intestinal upset of the first trip. I avoided any loose talk which might reveal that I bought guns for Indians.

When my usually sober-faced companions saw the amount of trade goods brought from the trading post, they reacted with visible joy. My standing among them improved greatly, and when we returned to the village a big celebration ensued. During the days of celebrating, I noticed that Chief Shumu, a very reserved old man, showed more concern and relief than usual over our safe return to the village. For the first time I noticed how frail he really had become.

Soon after the return from this second trip to the trading post, the chief ordered the diets and purges in preparation for a session of dreaming together. It had been many months since we had gone to the forest for a group ceremony. From the care in preparation and a few remarks I overheard, I became aware that Chief Shumu planned something special this time.

A select group of twelve went late in the afternoon to the secluded place in the forest. Some of the older men and several of the best hunters were included. The rituals and chants seemed similar to those of previous occasions but somewhat more elaborate. From the opening chants, with the fragrant smoke and the evocation of the forest spirits, it became evident to me that the chief wanted to fix in my mind all of the important and essential conditions of the tribal life. An intense feeling of oneness within the group showed our dedication to the purpose of the old man.

I became very much aware of the fragile hand that moved the fan to carry the magic smoke to each of the dreamers as we settled into a quiet reverie of joint communion, savoring the fragrant incense in the stillness of the silent forest. A soft chant from the chief held our thoughts together on a common theme.

During these chants, vistas of the forest vegetation, fantastic forms and shapes in vivid blue-green shades of color, began to form in our minds. Soon, with the chief's evocative chants embellished by the others, a procession of animals began in our dreams, starting with the jungle cats. Some of these I had not seen before in the dreams. Moving with stealth, the tawny puma, several varieties of the smaller spotted ocelot, and then a giant rosette-spotted jaguar passed. A murmur from the dreamers indicated recognition from previous dreams. This tremendous animal shuffled along with his head hanging down, mouth open, and tongue lolling out. He seemed harmless even with the large teeth that filled his hideous mouth. But an instant change in the animal's attitude to one of vicious alertness caused a tremor to pass through our circle of phantom-dreamers.

Stimulated by seeing this great cat, there came to my mind the memory of my experience years before when, alone on a rubber trail, I had confronted the large black jaguar. Now I chanted in the Huni Kui language, *"Ino, Ino Mosho"* (Black Jaguar) and the mighty black beast then intruded into the joint dreams of our group. A sigh passed through the circle as the dreamers realized that their apprentice shaman had for a moment taken over the direction of our dreams. As before, the demon of the forest blinked his eyes, turned his head and disappeared.

Then the chief's chanting brought a parade of other animals, birds, and snakes to our dreams, each with some detail important to the Huni Kui in dominating the forest.

Next came scenes of combat with the hated enemy, the Macaw people (Kana Tashi or Shaawo), a procession of the feared white-robed and hooded Bolanshos, and encounters with the Kiriwa and Kiruana, the hated invading rubber cutters. In one dream a village of the Huni Kui appeared in flames as the people scattered in panic into the forest. Here Chief Shumu, then a much younger man, killed a rubber cutter in violent hand-to-hand fighting. Scenes in the new village where we now lived gradually brought the dreams to an end. We awoke to shafting sunlight and morning birdsong penetrating our minds and the place of our dreams.

It is not possible to satisfactorily describe the deep feeling of unity shared by a group that has been through a session of dreaming together. I felt deep within myself a great sense of oneness with these people in their struggle to dominate the forces of nature for their daily living and to defend themselves against their enemies. We all returned to the village in a quiet mood.

Everyone seemed aware of the source of the black jaguar in our dreams. It left a strong impression on them, and they gave me the name of Ino Mosho, Black Jaguar. These people had a strong suspicion against the use of proper names for each other. Everyone had a private name, but it was never used in their daily life. They felt that to speak a person's real name made him vulnerable to evil spirits and bad luck. Instead they used nicknames. Many of the men went by the names of the animals they hunted or by a name taken from some unusual incident in their life. The women were often called simply "little sister," "cousin," "aunt," "old mother," or some nickname from things they did especially well. I, too, now had a nickname. Before the black panther visions, the Huni Kui sometimes had called me Moci Bira, Good Shooter, from my use of the rifle. Now, they all called me Ino Mosho.

16

Transition

How I Became Chief

AN OCCASIONAL APPREHENSIVE word or remark among the old women who took care of Chief Shumu's daily needs drew my attention to the fact that the chief was eating practically nothing, only a mouthful or two of fruit gruel a day. Nor did he sleep. Any time in the night when I roused from sleep I found Chief Shumu sitting in his hammock, gazing into the fire. The old women took turns sitting up with him.

The people around the ancient and fragile chief showed no special emotion toward him, but there was a feeling of constant watchfulness among those near him the old man.

One afternoon as I walked with the chief between the houses of the village, the old man's leg crumpled and he fell to the ground. The old women came in an instant at my shout. A wail went up from the women, but the old man silenced them with a sharp command. They carried him gently to his hammock and tried to make him comfortable. Their examination of the leg showed nothing wrong below the hip, but the hip bone must have broken.

As the word passed, the villagers gathered around, grim-faced and silent. Chief Shumu sent them all away, allowing only the old women to remain near to do what they could for him. The village, ordinar-

ily bustling with sound and activity, settled into a gloomy silence. That night a *chieu-chieu* bird flew around the house. The men half-heartedly lit fires and burned chili peppers to try to drive away the carrier of ill omen. The next day the chief would eat nothing and turned his face away without response when anyone spoke to him.

In the middle of the night a mournful wail broke out when the old women became aware that Chief Shumu's spirit had departed from his earthly body. Soon the whole village took up a low mournful chant which continued through the night.

The next morning the men built a low platform just off the floor. On this the old women laid out the chief in the dark house. A small torch of burning resin at one corner of the platform illuminated the scene as the men and women whom he had led for so many years gathered to mourn Chief Shumu's death.

The mourning alternated between chants and stories about the life and exploits of the chief. The older men and women told stories of his fighting and hunting abilities as a young man. Many tales centered around the arrival of the rubber cutters with firearms and their attempts to make the Indians work at rubber production. It took hours to recount the story of the final massacres that destroyed their villages on the Tarauaca River and the leadership of the old man in moving the remnants of the tribe to the center of the forest where they now lived. Many different men, and women too, added their individual episodes to the story.

As the mourning continued, several of the women began preparing wide strips of bark cloth from the inner bark of the *envira* tree. They hung these to dry over the fire. On the second day after Chief Shumu's death, the old women began to wrap his body with the strips of cloth. Beginning at the feet, they carefully wrapped the whole body to the head. Then they drew the body high up into the smoke-filled rafters of the house, using vine ropes. For several months, it hung there out of sight.

The usual village life came to a standstill and remained that way for days after Shumu's death. Men and women wandered about aimlessly or gathered in small groups to talk. The children also remained subdued. Chief Shumu had managed the people in many subtle ways. Awareness of his presence had been enough to keep the village operating efficiently. Now there was a terrible hole in the fabric of village life. For me, Chief Shumu had been like a second father and more. Now I felt a great aching loss. Added to the pain of this loss was the uncertainty of how the tribe expected me to fill the void left by the death of their chief.

Not until all the food in the village had been consumed did gathering start again, and then only gradually. The women began first by going to their gardens, as directed by the chief's old women. They brought back bananas, peanuts, corn, and yams from which they made the gruel that they called *mingau*. Soon after, the hunters started bringing in game again. Gradually, something like the old village life returned.

The Indians had not yet begun to look to me for direction. They intended, it turned out, to wait until the old chief was buried before reorganizing village life under a new chief.

When all the natural signs were right, the chief's old women started molding and firing several large clay urns. The clay came from a nearby deposit of gray earth that made excellent pots when molded and fired. When they had the urns ready, the old women lowered the body from the rafters where it had become a mummy in the hot, dry, smoky air. It was as stiff as a tree trunk.

With mournful chants and great reverence, the women unwrapped the mummy. Then with a specially prepared mixture of animal fats and palm-kernel oil, they began to rub the joints. Soon this softened the knees, hips, and elbows enough so they could double up the hard shriveled body into a sitting position, the knees drawn up under the chin. Into the most perfect of the urns the old women then placed

131

the body along with all of Chief Shumu's possessions. These included his ceremonial bow and arrows, a dance baton, the feather-decorated shirt, and many other things, as well as food. A second urn was then placed over the mouth of the burial urn, and the joint between the two was sealed with melted tree resin.

The men, women, and children all joined in the wailing songs and chants as they carried the urn to a deep hole prepared at the edge of the village clearing. Here it was buried, and seeds for food plants were planted around the grave. They carefully tended these plants and started new ones when needed. Doing this, they believed the departed spirit of their chief never lacked for food.

After the burial the village certainly did not forget Chief Shumu, but the mood of the tribe changed. A certain briskness in taking up the tribal activities became noticeable, a briskness that had been missing during the months following the chief's death. Within a few days after the burial, several of the men came to me and said I should lead them in a session of dreaming together so that their hunting skill would come back to normal. This was for me a new undertaking, a challenge, and a test.

I prepared the purges and specified the diets for cleansing their bodies for the ceremony as Chief Shumu had taught me. When all had been done to my satisfaction, we had our faces painted and went one afternoon to the glade in the forest to commune with the spirits.

On the way, the traditional chants came to me naturally, and I dispelled any fear my companions might feel over the new situation. The ceremony around the fire with the fragrant smoke went well and created the right mood of calm, enchanted expectation. The evocative dream chants I had learned also came easily to me, and I controlled the progress of the dreams. Along with the other forest cats the black jaguar appeared again when called by the chants. For the first time I had the feeling of leaving my body and actually traveling with the black panther. Many strange and marvelous dreams revealed

phantoms we had not seen before. In the morning the awakened dreamers discussed the wonderful things they had seen and expressed a strong feeling of satisfaction. They all seemed sure that now things would go well. This good feeling soon became apparent in the village after the ceremony. It created the impression that life would continue to go as smoothly as it had before.

By this time it had been over a year since we had been out to trade caucho for supplies. Many requests came to me for machetes and axes. We still did not have enough of the tools to go around. Since tools made work in the gardens much easier, all the people wanted their own.

Organization of caucho production provided good activity for keeping many men occupied. They began the work with enthusiasm, speculating on what they would get in return when the rubber went to the trading post.

It took several weeks to produce a caravan load of rubber blocks the right size and shape for backpacking. When the blocks were ready, I began selecting the crew that would accompany me to the Brazilian border to trade. Also, I had to organize the village for protection while I was gone. I left instructions with the old women to prepare a good batch of fermented liquor for our return celebration. Early one morning our caravan started off to the north with the rubber blocks.

This trip passed without special incident. I took care to organize advance scouting to avoid possible points of danger. When I arrived at the trading post, the people there were surprised that I had been away so long. Mr. Rodrigues told me that the rubber price had dropped nearly one-half while I had been away.

I had brought in over a ton of rubber, but with the price reduction only a small cash balance remained for deposit after my purchases were paid for. Rodrigues, however, assured me that the large cash balance already on hand from past trips was safe for as long as I wanted to leave it on deposit.

By sunset I was back at the landing in the forest with my purchases. We soon organized the loads and started for home. Two days out from the village I sent a runner ahead to announce our arrival. The celebration of the trading party's return turned into two days and nights of wild dancing and drinking. Toward the end, long-standing domestic and inter-family feuds and conflicts began to show up among the men. I found that my understanding of the background of these fights was not really good enough for me to settle them to everyone's satisfaction. I needed more experience. It would take me a long time to develop the control that had seemed so easy when old Chief Shumu had been in charge.

In order to understand better how the people I now led interacted with each other to function as a village society, I began a series of sessions of dreaming together. One of the chief's old women suggested this to me as a way of understanding quickly. I selected a group of the important older men of the village and instructed them in the diets and purges they should follow to prepare their bodies.

When all was ready, I led the group to the sanctuary in the forest. Using the sad and eerie chants learned from Chief Shumu I led the men through a series of fantastic dreams, and I began to realize that the dreams seemed to obey these songs and chants. I tested this idea in the next session several days later. I chanted what I wanted to dream about. I found the dreams that came followed the wishes I expressed in my song. In succeeding attempts, this leading of the dreams became easier and easier.

Once the men realized that I had achieved domination over their dreams, they considered me a true magician, a position superior to theirs. At the same time, I developed a more acute awareness and understanding of my surroundings and the people about me by means of the dreams. This helped me to anticipate any difficult situation and be alert to handle it smoothly.

Toward the end of the series of dream sessions, I began to plan in

advance what we should examine in our dreams. I then expressed this in the chants and song, and dreams appeared as desired. I was able to greatly increased my knowledge and understanding of tribal lore and methods of preparing cures from plant materials and developing uses for these herbal medicines. Because of this, I began to improve both the preparation of the medicinal extracts and their use.

135

This soon became known to the people in the tribe, and it made my position even stronger in the village.

Through their customary preventive use of herbal preparations, the Huni Kui remained a healthy and vigorous people. Sickness among them was unusual, but when someone did fall ill, everyone became upset and worried until they saw the person well again. They believed sickness came from *Iushibo,* an evil spirit entering the body through witchcraft. A cure required witchcraft stronger than the offending spirit.

They told me, "The moon, sun, and stars never kill us, young or old. Only the evil spirits have it in their power to make us die and disappear. The gods are the heavenly bodies that illuminate us. They control the evil spirits and can send them to punish us."

When someone became ill, it fell to me to send away the offending spirit. Chief Shumu had prepared me for this role, and I used his methods.

These people believed that the most powerful human force came from their shaman's breath, and words coming from this breath had a creative force. Thus, with evocative chants and fragrant smoke coming from my pipe filled with tobacco and other herbs, I could create a trance-like mood around the sick one. At the end of the healing ceremony, I would forcefully blow the fragrant smoke over the body. If symptoms of pain were present, I would suck out the offending thorns from the body and by sleight of hand, prepared in advance, show them to the patient. This intensive treatment with the patient in a hypnotic trance initiated the desired cure. Herbal baths and oral potions completed the healing.

17

Frustration

On Why They Wanted Me Confined to the Village

THE HUNI KUI that I now led controlled the area at the headwaters of the Jurua, Purus, Madre de Dios, Michagua, and Inuya Rivers in Peru. Our extended village was scattered along a range of hills at the headwaters of the De Las Piedras River, a tributary of the Madre de Dios River. This is still the most isolated part of the Amazon River valley. The Indians named this place Shanada (The Place to Begin Again) when they settled here, away from all navigable streams, to avoid contact with the invading rubber cutters. From this refuge they made raids to avenge attacks made on them in the past, both by rubber cutters and by other Indian tribes.

Some of my men were violent in nature and seemed to live only to fight and make trouble. It became clear to me after Chief Shumu died that these men would not be easy to manage. I saw that some of them preferred to do as they pleased and organize things among themselves. I became aware that a small group from some nearby houses had been absent for several days and had come back with material taken in a raid on a rubber camp somewhere. One of the old women came to me with a complaint that the men were not sharing the things they brought back. Then rather slyly, she reminded

me that once before I had objected to raiding rubber camps. She hinted that if I were to control the tribe, I would have to make the men follow my wishes.

That same day I asked some of the old women to prepare the liquid tobacco extract and I sent word for the men to gather the next day for a tobacco talk. By midday the group had gathered in the chief's house where the shallow dish of tobacco extract sat on the floor. As before, when this kind of discussion had taken place under Chief Shumu, the men sat in a circle and the dish was passed around so that each person could dip his finger in for a few drops to put on his tongue. The discussion started quietly. In the calmest manner possible I went over what Chief Shumu had taught me and what had been done to get arms and trade goods for the tribe.

Gradually the others entered into the discussion, with related and unrelated comments. After several hours of conversation, I told the group I was aware that some of them were going off on distant hunting trips without instructions. By indirect allusion to the subject I let the men know that I knew what kind of game they were hunting and what they had brought back to the village. Then I told them that if it continued, evil spirits and disastrous times would destroy the tribe. I reminded them that Chief Shumu had brought them to this isolated place away from all the big rivers so that they could avoid contact with the rubber cutters, not use it as a place to organize raids on them.

The men responded that the rubber cutters were withdrawing from some of the areas they had previously occupied and that the tribe still lacked revenge for many attacks when relatives had been killed and children stolen. After an involved and wandering discussion, one of the old men suggested that I go with a group of them on an expedition back to Hoonwa-ia, the Tarauaca River, the far-off place from which they had come many years ago with Chief Shumu. By making this trek in reverse, they thought I would reach a better understanding of their attitude toward the rubber cutters. This seemed important to them and provided a way around the block our discussion had reached.

I knew that I could not expect my people to easily and quickly change an attitude based on such deep emotions. The expedition they proposed offered an experience that would unify the tribe. So I consented and took the initiative in ordering the preparations and selecting the party to make the trip.

I purposely chose a mixed group that included some of the older men who had made the original migration, some of the people they had found at the new location and joined with to form the present tribe, and some of the young hunters born since the founding of the village. Also, I organized and instructed a guard group to stay behind to protect the village. I told the old women to prepare a batch of liquor for the celebration of our return.

It took several days to prepare provisions for the trip—smoking meat, boiling and roasting yucca, and drying cakes made of ground corn and peanuts. During this time of preparation, the people spent evenings around the fire, going over every detail they could remember of events that had caused their migration and what took place on the trip.

At dawn on a cool morning, with mist drifting among the houses at Shanada, our party of twenty men departed toward the north. The first day we traveled rapidly through familiar territory. In late afternoon our leader stopped at a place they said had been their last camp before coming to the site chosen by Chief Shumu for their present village, Shanada.

Here we made camp, and around the fire one of the older men told me how Chief Shumu had first scouted with a small group of three or four to find an isolated location where they could live in peace. He had done this after gathering the remnants of the tribe together in the forest, following a series of disastrous battles with rubber cutters. Nishi was the only one left who had come with Chief

Shumu on his scouting expedition to locate the new village site. Nishi was too old now to make the long trek and had been left behind to help guard the village.

After another day's travel, we stopped for the night at another of the campsites, and a different episode of the migration was described. Finally, after several days, the group arrived at the place where the people said Chief Shumu had gathered them together in the forest to heal the wounded and organize the migration.

They told me how, while the refugees had been camped in this place so long ago, one of the hunters came upon a tremendous boa, *donowan owapashoni,* while hunting in the forest nearby. They considered this a sign of great good luck because the people venerated the boa. It heartened the small band of refugees, and they gathered around to sing and dance. Afterward they killed the boa and ate its flesh to capture its spirit. From the skin they made headbands to give them continuing good luck.

From here Chief Shumu had gone out to find a safe place to start the new village. When he found the location, he encountered people nearby who spoke the Huni Kui language—the Shabo and Ishabo, Palm Tree people. With great eloquence, Chief Shumu convinced these people that the group of stragglers he was bringing would cause no trouble. In the beginning there actually was much trouble, but Chief Shumu had finally brought them all together in harmony as one tribe, the Donowan. The Boa and the Palm Tree clans united and called their Place to Begin Again Shanada.

Now at the boa camp the travelers made shelters, and with a small group I went to visit the sites of the various villages on the Tarauaca River that had been destroyed by the rubber cutters. The attacks had come at dawn from the river. Large groups of attackers had arrived in canoes, all well armed with rifles. They had routed the surprised villagers, killing many of them as they fled into the forest. The Indians had no defense but flight, for the bow and arrow is no match for a repeating rifle in a cleared area. The few invaders who followed the Indians into the forest were killed by swift silent arrows. I heard many stories of atrocities committed by the rubber cutters.

In the general area of the Indian villages, the rubber cutters had established camps for themselves after the Indians had fled. Now these were nearly all abandoned and falling apart, the clearings growing up to forest again. The Indians wondered about this and asked me about it. My answer revealed nothing of my real thoughts. In my own mind I remembered what I had heard about falling rubber prices at the trading post on my last trip there. I said nothing about this to my Indians.

We did find one location still occupied by rubber cutters. The Indians tried to convince me to attack and kill these hated invaders. In the end I was able to convince them that this would only bring trouble for Shanada, at a time when they already had enough problems standing off the Macaw people and the other Indian invaders of our territory.

One night at the boa camp I dreamt of trouble back at Shanada. The next morning we broke camp and started home by forced march. In a few days we arrived back at our refuge on the hills in the center of the forest. There was great rejoicing at our return. Signs that our territory was being invaded had again been found. One young hunter had disappeared in the forest and had been neither seen nor heard from again.

Nishi, who had been left in charge, assured me that there was no immediate danger. No one could openly attack the village as long as my people had firearms. I sent out patrols and found that the invaders had apparently retreated. So there was no reason for canceling the return celebration as long as we maintained a guard. Body painting soon got under way, and when it was completed, the singing and dancing started as drinks were passed around. During the wild second day of the celebration, several fights broke out among the men

over trivial things. By this time I understood better the incidents causing the trouble and settled the disputes more easily than before.

A few days later, I began talks with Nishi and several of the other older men about trying to discover where the invasion of our forest was coming from. The young man who had disappeared had not been found nor his loss avenged, and this caused tension in the village. It seemed to these older men that the invasion came from the southwest. Several patrols were sent out in that direction. They all came back with no evidence of a target for an attack in retaliation.

To occupy my people's minds, I again organized caucho rubber production. Several months later we took a good load of rubber blocks to the trading post. The price had dropped again and Rodrigues mentioned that rubber cutters were leaving the forest. The caucho I had brought just barely covered the cost of the things I wanted to buy. A nagging doubt entered my mind about the future of trading caucho for goods. The Indians were becoming accustomed to having some of the things they could get only through me at the trading post, especially arms, ammunition, and metal tools. This was important to my influence and power over them.

When we returned back to the village, I found the wild drinking and dancing distasteful for the first time, but dared not show it. I had learned from Chief Shumu that it was the place of the chief to show no personal reaction to any situation except under very special conditions when he wanted to create a counterreaction from the people.

Now I found myself spending more time than usual in the forest, trying to use up my excess energy and help relieve my feeling of tension over the falling rubber prices. In this way I became more familiar with the details of the tribal hunting territory, and it was possible for me to organize the hunting activities of the men more effectively. One day out hunting I had gone down the bank of a small creek and started climbing up the other side when a large arrow buried itself in the earth at my side. Immediately I dodged behind a tree and blew a high-pitched whistle I always carried on a string around my neck. The Indians had given me this whistle to use as a danger signal to call for help after the last ambush. In a few minutes some of the hunters arrived, and they organized a search while one man went back to the village to get more help. When the villagers arrived, an escort took me back, while the rest began an intensive search for the attacker.

At sundown they came in, chanting and carrying between them a man bound to a pole. The men tied the captive to the owl tree between the houses and kindled a small fire nearby. Then the entire village came to taunt and screech their rage at the captive. Nishi requested that the prisoner be held until the following day. He wanted to work on the captive in daylight to get the maximum amount of information from him about our enemies. I set up an all-night guard to watch and protect the prisoner.

In the morning a shout rang out! To everyone's surprise the captive hung dead in his bonds. No mark of violence or wounds showed on the body. The guards had perhaps dozed off, but they had heard nothing happen. The Indians told me that the man had died of his own will. They explained that this was possible but seldom in such a short time.

Now came the question of what to do about the body. All agreed it should be taken out into the forest far enough away so the smell would not come back to the village, and left there for the buzzards. They considered this the worst possible fate. Several men then carried it away to a place Nishi and I agreed on. When we checked on the body a week later, not a sign remained, not even a bone. This was a very bad omen. It meant that someone had carried the remains away. Who did it? Who watched us so closely here in the depths of our own territory?

Again, scouting parties went out to try and determine where the assassination attempts came from. The results were uncertain, and tension again built up in the village. I had to invent projects to divert attention from the trouble.

We started to produce another shipment of caucho. Several weeks later I went out into the forest to check on how many blocks of rubber were ready. I went off quite a distance from the men to look at a fruit tree nearly ready to attract game. When I turned to go back, an arrow came flying through the air from a distant clump of underbrush. It had been a long shot and I grabbed the arrow as it floated by, most of its force spent. At once I shot into the vegetation from where the arrow seemed to come, and then signaled an alarm with my whistle.

An organized search this time produced nothing, not a sign to go by. At this news, the entire village turned grim-faced and frustrated, ready to fight but with nothing to attack.

A group of the old men led by Nishi came to me and asked that I stay in the village, except when carefully escorted. They insisted that when I went off alone in the forest they could not protect me. To be armed with a rifle was not protection. One could not see far enough. Our enemy had become aware of the firepower at Shanada and was trying to eliminate the source of our arms—me. The men said that if I could tell them where the attacks were coming from they would go destroy the enemy. Nishi suggested that perhaps by dreaming I could locate the source of trouble.

I tried staying in the village for a few weeks, and I became desperate. It was well enough for an old man like ancient Chief Shumu to stay in the village. But I was now barely twenty years old and at the peak of good health and vigor, and I could not stand it. I had to find some way to use up my energy. To be confined to the village all the time was the same as being in jail. Around this time I began to notice again the smell of the Indians—a strange, persistent musky odor that was especially strong inside the houses at night. I came to dislike it very much.

18

Escape and Return

My Reaction to Confinement

SEEKING SOME WAY to escape confinement in the village, I decided in desperation to try to locate our enemies by dreaming as Nishi had suggested. This time I would dream alone. I had done this before, but with Chief Shumu watching over and guiding me. I started to prepare with the usual diet and purges, but for some reason these preliminaries made me irritable. I had to hide any sign of this from my companions. Then I ordered the small shelter made ready at the edge of the forest.

Late one afternoon about an hour before sundown, Owa Iushabo, Old Mother, went with me into the forest to watch over me during the dreaming. Guards had already been sent into the forest out of sight to watch against any intrusion. The trilling notes of a birdcall in reply to my own signals told me that the guards were at their posts.

Chanting to myself, I built a small fire and put on the leaves. As the fragrant smoke filled the area with its incense, I poured and drank a cup of the magic fluid from the vine and sat down in a small hammock. There I closed my eyes and awaited the beginning of the dreams. A flight of blue and red macaws went over at tree top level. Their raucous, strident calls echoed through the forest, shattering

the calm peace of the late afternoon and creating a feeling of menace and danger.

In reaction to the noise, I broke out in a sweat and felt nauseated. I groped in my mind for some way to gain control of my thoughts and feelings, but the chants for this failed to come. Images of brilliant blue and green forms began to appear in my mind as the dreams started. Then distorted faces intruded as the bright colors faded. As these faces became clearer I recognized them as those of my family back in Iquitos. Then I realized that there was sickness—my mother lay dying in her bed. Feelings of unbearable sadness took over my dream as I realized that I would never see my mother again.

Next I found myself wandering alone in a forest of gigantic trees. Rough misshapen boulders and twisting vines lurked everywhere on the uneven slippery ground. The sound of a strange birdcall held my attention. At the sound of a plucked bowstring, suddenly a huge feathered arrow came whizzing through the air. I stood transfixed, unable to move. The missile struck me down, and a hideous, grimacing savage stepped from behind a tree. Vivid red paint covered the massive body of my attacker. Deliberately he came and put a naked foot on my chest as my life's blood ebbed out onto the ground. Then I had visions of my body left unburied in the forest, ravaged by buzzards and carrion animals.

Meaningless images followed for a time. Then came the sublime face of Chief Shumu gazing at me. With this moving vision, I regained control of my dreams. The black panther appeared, and the two of us became one, wandering the forest together afraid of nothing.

I awoke in the gray dawn there in the edge of the forest, the fire still glowing, attended by Old Mother. She was staring at me, a troubled look only half hidden on her face. I felt exhausted, barely able to move. The old woman approached my hammock with a bowl of fruit drink. She had to hold my head up so I could drink. I then struggled to a sitting position with her help. She grumbled some half-heard, disapproving remark.

The final dream of Chief Shumu and the black panther were all that gave me the strength to return to the village. Even so it took me until almost midday before I had gained enough control of myself to face the villagers. Many birdcalls passed back and forth, but the guards did not intrude. I knew that I had to appear to the people in the village, outwardly at least, the same when I came from the forest as when I had gone into it the afternoon before. Inwardly, my dreams of my mother dying left me with a feeling of utter shock and despair. These feelings I could share with no one.

Finally Old Mother and I walked slowly and calmly from the forest. I made my face into the the mask I had learned to show the people. I told them only that I had dreamed of Chief Shumu. And I entered again the village routine of directing the daily activities of the tribe.

As the days passed, the feeling of depression from the dream eased somewhat. But at night my dreams returned as terrible nightmares. Whenever I talked or shouted in my sleep, one of the old women near me would light a torch and awaken me to chase away the evil spirits. To avoid disturbing the others in the house with my sleep-talking, I forced myself to sleep only fitfully and to awaken when the dreams started. Of course this only increased my nervous tension. And now the musky smell of the closed house at night made the situation worse than ever.

In desperation, I organized a group to cut caucho again and went with them into the forest. They took elaborate care to protect me, but did not object as long as I stayed within the group for protection. I put forth great physical effort to ease my inner tension.

When we had the shipment of rubber ready, I organized the trip to the trading post. There I learned the depressing news that rubber prices had continued to fall, and rubber cutters were still leaving the forest. I found the stock of merchandise at the trading post very low.

Some of the things I wanted were not available. Rodrigues told me a new shipment of goods was expected from Manaus in about three months when the river rose with the coming rainy season. I tried to find some way to fix that point of time in my mind.

The money from the caucho barely covered a few knickknacks. I drew from my balance on deposit to make the purchases seem large enough to impress my companions. They wanted more firearms, but I had in mind a reason for not buying any at this time.

Back where my men waited in the forest on the riverbank I explained that new arms were on the way, but had not yet reached the trading post. I told them the new guns would be much better than the ones we had now. With them we would have better defense against our enemies. Since the Indians found the rifles, except for the noise they made, not much more effective than their bows and arrows in the forest, the news of improved arms was exciting to them.

We went home to Shanada and had the usual big celebration. This relieved tension in the tribe but did not help me. Soon the natural signs of the approaching rainy season began to appear. The rains would make caucho production difficult. A few blocks had been left behind when we had made up the loads for our last trip. By alternating work groups and much urging I managed to get enough loads together for a trip before the heavy rains started. I kept thinking of the supply launch that was expected at the trading post and how I could be there when it arrived.

This time I left the village with a feeling of great sadness that I dared not let show. My wife Huaini and son Iria, now a vigorous growing boy, sensed that something was wrong and clung to me briefly at our departure. The trip turned into a nightmare. Sporadic rains had started before we departed, and two days out on the trail we were caught in a deluge. At mid-morning distant thunder sounded off to the east. This continued off and on until midday, when a strong breeze hit the forest making even the large trees sway. The wind penetrated to the forest floor and cooled our bodies. This did not please my Indians, however. Apprehension showed on their faces and muttering complaints passed around in the group.

All of a sudden the wind stopped. It became deathly silent with not a sign of air movement. Darkness became more intense on the already shaded forest floor. Soon a steady far-off roar started and grew louder in a crescendo as a downpour of rain moved across the treetops toward us. It turned darker before the roar actually reached us. The darkness was broken by indistinct blue flashes of lightning that penetrated the vegetation. The wind began again, and explosions of thunder sounded over the roar of the approaching rain.

As if by command, a great deluge of water came cascading through the forest. Wind, rain, thunder, and flashes of blue light combined to cause great confusion. Suddenly the wind increased. Huge trees began to sway and groan. Nearby we could hear the frightening, awesome sound of shattered, crashing tree trunks.

The Indians moved instinctively to a small rise in the land covered mostly by small trees. Large trees came crashing down all around us, and water rose fast in the lowland around the small hill. We huddled together in fear. The shattering wind passed on as fast as it had come, but the rain diminished only gradually.

The next morning, daylight revealed a forest in chaos. Off to the left appeared a strip of jungle completely blown down, with large twisted and broken trees lying on top of one another. Luckily we had been only on the edge of it. The Indians were shaken by the experience and muttered about evil spirits.

Traveling with packloads through the forest after such a heavy rain was nearly impossible. The ground underfoot turned into a quagmire. As delays held us back on the trail, my tension mounted. I had bad dreams at night during my fitful, troubled sleep. I kept seeing a launch navigating up a swift crooked stream. It would come into sight, then fade into the thick green vegetation. As I strained to catch another sight of it I would wake up, cramped and sore from sitting in my tiny leafed shelter with the rain dripping through.

Finally, after a brutal struggle through the sodden jungle with our loads of rubber, we arrived one night at our usual staging area in the forest above the trading post. Exhausted and apprehensive, we made a small raft. At daylight I started poling the raft with blocks of rubber strung out behind on a vine rope downriver, toward the cluster of houses on the bank below the bend in the river. I told my companions that I would be back before sundown, as always.

At the trading post Rodrigues greeted me with surprise. "You used to come only once a year, or even less often. Now you are back after only a few weeks."

He had just finished checking off the cargo from a launch in port at the trading post. I asked when it would leave.

"When the fuel wood has been loaded, probably about midnight," he replied. " Why?"

My answer was to ask to have my caucho weighed in.

"It's not worth much." came the reply. "If prices keep on as they are, I am going to shut this place down and return to Manaus."

To Manaus! To Manaus! The idea echoed in my head.

Manaus, an enchanting faraway place that I had heard about in Iquitos. To Manaus?

I helped weigh in the blocks of rubber, and as we worked, a wild idea kept forming in my mind. Or perhaps it had been there for some time and was now surfacing again. The money for the load of rubber hardly seemed worth counting. I took some from my balance on deposit there at the trading post to buy things I knew my people would find attractive. But I bought no guns or ammunition.

When the purchases were packaged for the trip back, I asked permission to use a canoe to take the purchases upstream. In reply Rodrigues asked if I wanted a man to go with me to bring the canoe back.

I had been struggling with wild thoughts. The question decided the point for me. "No," I said, "I'll bring it back myself. Is there space for a passenger on the launch?"

"It is empty—all yours, if you wish. Why? Where are you going?" asked Rodrigues.

"I will be back before dark. Prepare a statement of my balance on deposit. I will take it with me to Manaus," I replied.

Paddling the canoe upriver with the things for the Indians seemed to take forever. I thought about the assassination attempts on my life by the tribe's enemies trying to eliminate my people's source of protective firearms. I wondered how, with the rubber prices falling, I would be able to buy guns and the other things my people had become accustomed to having. All this could affect my influence over the people and my ability to lead them. Then I remembered the visions of my mother dying and my compelling desire to rejoin my family in Iquitos. My family ties there had been strong ones.

When I arrived at the beach, I could tell that the Indians noticed I was alone. They helped me unload the canoe in silence. As we prepared the carrying loads I showed them the items, hoping to please them.

Then I said, "New rifles are being unloaded now at the trading post. They are the guns I told you about. They will shoot through the trees. The trees will not stop our bullets any more. They will kill our enemies who hide behind the trees. These new arms are being unpacked tonight. There are many people waiting now to buy these guns. If I am not there to buy them for us, our enemies the rubber cutters will buy them all."

Muttering passed through the waiting group.

"I am going back there now," I told them. "I will get the new guns for us that will shoot through the trees and kill the enemies that hide from us. Tomorrow at midday I will bring them here. You will see. To be safe from discovery until I come, you must take all this to our camp in the forest and return tomorrow."

They grumbled and hesitated. A small canoe appeared on the river below. This brought action and stopped all discussion as they hurriedly evacuated the riverbank.

I reassured them once more and departed in my canoe. As I slowly drifted downriver the plaintive call of the tinamou floated on the evening air out of the forest where my men had just disappeared. How should I fathom its intent? It was a signal we had used on occasion as a warning.

Back at the trading post, I bought some clothing, a hammock, and received from Rodrigues the statement of my account, before boarding the launch. Both on shore and on the launch I was offered food but refused because of past stomach upsets. A feeling of total numbness filled my body as I searched out a corner of the deck where I could be alone. It seemed the launch would never leave—a thousand last-minute details and instructions had to be passed. Rodrigues came on board and tried to engage me in conversation by asking more questions. These I put off somehow and finally was left alone.

The hiss of escaping steam as boiler pressure built up indicated our pending departure. At last, in a shower of sparks, hissing steam, several hoots on the steam whistle, and with the throbbing of the engine, the launch eased out into a swift current of the flooded river.

I felt numb in mind and body from weeks of great physical effort and nervous tension. Now I could relax. Even so, a tumult of thoughts about the past and the future flooded my mind until I slept from utter exhaustion. My hammock swayed with the motion of the launch. On either side of the river the thick green jungle vegetation hung down over the swift muddy water. If a small tinamou awoke in the night and called from the depths of the forest I did not hear it. As I slept there in my swaying hammock in a secluded corner of the deck, the thrust of both the launch and the current of the Purus River carried me downstream away from the depths of the forest, toward Manaus, the fabled capital of the Amazon.

From the trading post on the Peru-Brazil border the Purus River wanders through the Amazon forest, doubling back on itself a thousand times before reaching the Amazon River near Manaus. The trip downriver was taking me back to my former life, and I began another time of difficult adjustment. The confinement of the launch on the long journey seemed as bad or worse than that of the Indian village. Wearing clothing again became an irritating necessity. Remembering how sick I had been after eating at the trading post, I avoided the launch food at first. By eating mostly bananas and plantains the first few days, I eased slowly into eating the highly seasoned diet of my new associates.

Talking with the launch crew and the passengers picked up at other trading posts on the way downriver proved difficult at first. My native tongue, Peruvian Spanish, unused for the past few years, seemed to me almost a foreign language. My Spanish came back, but slowly. It had some similarities to the Portuguese spoken in Brazil. In this border region both languages were understood to some extent by most people. By the time the launch reached Manaus, after two weeks or so of downriver travel, I could make myself understood fairly well. The people on board were all curious about the unknown stranger, but I told them nothing about my recent experiences. I had no way of knowing what the reaction of my Indian people would be to my disappearance. No doubt it would be violent. The people at the trading post were in danger. I could not have warned them, however, without making my departure impossible. All this caused me great distress, which I could share with no one.

On the trip I had plenty of time to think about the past and wonder about the future. Thinking back, I realized that from the very moment of my capture I had instinctively sought to understand and gain control over the strange world into which I had been drawn. As my understanding developed, I naturally tried to shape events to my own advantage. Every trip from the isolation of the forest out to the trading post had increased the tension and conflicts between my new and my former life. My early family ties had been strong, and for this reason I probably never completely gave up the idea of escape and return. When the first real chance came in all those years of captivity, it seemed inevitable that I took advantage of it to return to my own people.

Now that I had indeed escaped, I wondered what I would find on arrival, home in Iquitos. How would I fit into that other life I had left so long ago?

The day did finally arrive when the launch tied up to the dock at Manaus. I was totally unprepared for the confusion, the rushing and bustling of the busy seaport a thousand miles up the Amazon River. Fortunately, during the trip I had made friends with the mechanic's helper who agreed to go ashore with me and take me to the office of Luzero-Rodrigues da Costa & Company. There the balance on the rubber deliveries I had made upriver was to be paid.

At the office, Paulo Rodrigues da Costa had already heard of my arrival from the launch captain. When I gave him the statement of my account, Sr. Rodrigues asked me to return the next day and said that I could stay on the launch for the night if I wanted to. The next day at the office, Don Paulo asked, "What are your plans? Do you expect to buy supplies and return upriver?"

"No," I replied, "I am returning to Iquitos."

"What is your connection there?"

I explained that I had been outfitted by my brother-in-law, Lino Vela of Iberia. I explained that the balance on the statement from the trading post on the upper Purus was the profit from the grubstake, that I was returning to its owner, Lino Vela. Don Paulo found Lino listed in his record of rubber shippers in Peru. He had bought supplies from Luzero-Rodrigues in Manaus and his credit was good.

Then Don Paulo asked, "What can I do for you?"

I answered, "Arrange for my passage upriver to Iquitos as soon as

possible and give me the balance of the account in pound sterling notes." These British notes were the accepted means of exchange in the Amazon at that time.

In a couple of days I found myself on board a large steam launch on its way to Iquitos. Hesitatingly, I tried to find out something about my family from the Peruvian passengers on board, without results. Unfortunately, when I arrived in Iquitos, I found out that my dream in the Indian village had been true. My parents, along with many others, had died in an epidemic of what was then called the Spanish influenza. I had money in my pocket, but no home to go to.

It was now 1918 and World War I in Europe had just ended. The war had caused a temporary rise in rubber prices, and I soon found work running a rubber camp for the J. Borda Company in the forest of the Tapiche River, upcountry from Iquitos. This put me right back in the forest working with other Indian tribes like the Witoto and the Cocama. What I learned about life in the forest with the Huni Kui helped me protect myself after my escape. Trading in the rubber my new people produced for supplies at the Borda Company warehouse on the lower Tapiche River was not too different than what I had done on the Purus River with Luzero-Rodrigues da Costa Company. Of course I had to relearn the Spanish language, but that came easy.

19

Epilogue

On Becoming a Healer

I SOON BECAME dissatisfied with bachelor life and remarried. I took my wife, Nieves Ochoa, with me to the jungle rubber camp on the upper Tapiche River. There our two daughters were born. Before long the price of rubber fell again, so low that it became impossible for me to make a living in the forest. We returned to the town of Requena at the mouth of the Tapiche River on the main river called the Ucayali. I established a farm that prospered. As I adapted the knowledge of my former Indian captors, my healing power and skill soon became known in this region where doctors were few or nonexistent. The knowledge I had obtained from Chief Shumu about how to determine the cause of illness in people and how to treat it with medicinal plants from the forest proved invaluable.

On our farm, my two boys were born, and when the children came of school age, I sold my farm and moved to Iquitos where I myself had gone to school. My reputation as a healer followed me there. My success with healing people who were ill caused problems with the local doctors because I had no license to practice medicine. The situation became so difficult for awhile that I had to go into exile in Brazil. But I had powerful friends who had benefited from my

ability to heal. They soon arranged for my return home to Iquitos.

Many of the people I treated came to me after their medical doctors had told them their condition was incurable. When I made them well, people were inclined to call the result a miracle. I believe, however, that since man is a part of nature, the cure for all man's ills will be found in nature. The substances that Indian Chief Shumu taught me how to prepare and use to make people well all came from nature. I did not think that helping people in this way was at all miraculous.

In addition to countless river people of the Peruvian Amazon region, my patients included a former President of Peru, a Belgian Ambassador to Peru, and many Peruvian Army and Navy officers of the highest rank who found out about my ability to heal when they were stationed in the Amazon region of Peru. In recent years medical people have come to consult with me from Japan, Spain, Belgium, Colombia, and Argentina. Cures that I achieved in my years of healing service are ample testimony of their effectiveness and value.

Naturally, as the years passed, I wondered about the life of the Huni Kui and the family I had left behind. An occasional rumor from the depths of the jungle and the dreams in which I traveled with the black jaguar provided my only source of information about that strange primitive world. Recent reports from the Tahuamanu, Tamaya, De las Piedras, and Inuya Rivers indicate that the Huni Kui are still active in that region. Indians on the Inuya River who have been in recent contact with outsiders tell of a large, isolated village of people called the Rondowo, Snake People, who live on the upper Sepahua River, near the village of my captivity. They are reported to have a chief named Iriya who sometimes trades with outsiders. Perhaps this Iriya is my son Iria, now the new leader of the Huni Kui with whom I lived and from whom I learned so much.